# The Age of Television

Martin Esslin

*Stanford University*

W. H. Freeman and Company
San Francisco

This book was published originally as a part of *The Portable Stanford*, a series of books published by the Stanford Alumni Association, Stanford, California.

**Library of Congress Cataloging in Publication Data**

Esslin, Martin.
    The age of television.

    Bibliography: p.
    Includes index.
    1. Television broadcasting—Social aspects—United States.    I. Title.
PN1992.6.E87        302.2′3        81-12552
ISBN 0-7167-1337-3                AACR2
ISBN 0-7167-1338-1 (pbk.)

Printed in the United States of America

1  2  3  4  5  6 7  8  9  0    MP    8  9  8  7  6  5  4  3  2  1

# CONTENTS

# A PERSONAL PREFACE

This is a book about one of the most important, most neglected, and most underrated social phenomena of our time: television—its nature, impact, and long-term consequences, both positive and negative. It deals with television from a general point of view, but also takes most of its examples, including its targets for criticism, from where they lie nearest at hand and are most familiar to the readers of this book— from American television.

But as this book is by someone who is, at least in part, an outside observer of the American scene, my attempts to make a contribution to the debate may perhaps need a degree of explanation. And it is only fair that someone with strong opinions to unleash openly declare his background and bias from the outset.

I have spent the bulk of my adult and professional life in the electronic mass media in Britain. I worked, in various capacities, for the BBC from 1940 when I was twenty-one years old until I retired from the organization in 1977 as head of the radio drama department. I was thus nurtured in the atmosphere and philosophy of broadcasting as a public service. But having been involved in the internal problems and conflicts of public service broadcasting from the very outset of my career and in a managerial capacity for the last twenty years of my service with the BBC, I also became very critical of many of the aspects of this type of public service organization.

I began coming to the United States in the late 1950s after the publication of my first books and have become increasingly involved in American academic life, first as a lecturer and visiting professor, and, since 1977, after my retirement from the BBC, as professor of drama at Stanford University, which keeps me in California for six months of each year. Being interested professionally in the mass media and passionately concerned about their use, I became, inevitably, deeply immersed in looking—critically—at American television.

I thus see the medium both with the eyes of a detached outsider and with those of a concerned insider. American popular culture has become the popular culture of the world at large. American television is thus more than a purely local phenomenon. It fascinates—and in some instances frightens—the whole world.

To a native, American television as it is simply constitutes part of his or her natural environment. It is as unquestioned as the air he or she breathes (or less so, for air pollution has now become a national issue). Few Americans realize that their system of television is by no means the only one possible or acceptable. So perhaps there is a place for an outsider like myself, who is both sympathetic and concerned, to draw attention to features not only of the television scene in general but to that in the U.S. in particular that he finds significant, disturbing, or alarming. Yet let it be understood that any criticism advanced here springs from a basis of deep admiration for the U.S. and a conviction that its continued prosperity and power are of vital importance to the future of the world.

I should also at this point like to express my thanks for the great help I have had in the preparation of this book from The Portable Stanford and especially the editorial advice, challenge, and debate provided by Cynthia Fry Gunn, without whose aid this book would not have come into existence.

Martin Esslin

Stanford, California
February 28, 1981

*Spread of Thought* by Victor Brauner. Collection, The Solomon R. Guggenheim Museum, New York.

# 1

# The Drama Explosion

WALK THROUGH A SUBURBAN STREET in any developed country of the world, when the night is warm and the windows are open: in house after house you will see, shining through, the bluish flicker from a television screen. What would a visitor from a previous generation emerging from a time machine make of it—a whole population, locked in the contemplation of flickering images for hours on end, in passive receptivity, as though spellbound? Writing before the advent of television, Aldous Huxley imagined in *Brave New World* (1932) a dystopia of future populations drugged into acquiescence with tranquilizing pills. Huxley was not far off the mark, deficient only in the technological component of his prophetic vision. In an important sense his brave new world is with us: it is called "the age of television."

There can be no doubt that television has brought about a major revolution in the development of man's life-styles, culture, and social habits. We tend to think of revolutions as political events, violent overthrows of existing systems of government. But compared with technological and economic revolutions, which steal upon us almost unobserved, political revolutions have a far less profound impact. Upheavals like the Russian Revolution or the overthrow of the Shah in Iran leave much of the fabric of living unaffected; even political life often reverts to a pattern not far different from that under the previous regime. The taming of fire, on the other hand, or the invention of the wheel, Gutenberg's introduction of printing with movable type, or the coming of the steam engine and the age of rail transport have had deep and lasting effects on human life and thought. They have fundamentally altered mankind's way of perceiving reality.

On one level or another we are all aware that the coming of the television age, which can be dated roughly from 1950, marked just such a revolutionary turning point. But though the all-pervasive nature of the medium and its possible effects on manners and morals are debated constantly, the full implications of the change in human habits and modes of perception brought about by TV do not seem to have yet penetrated our consciousness.

As is so often the case with revolutionary developments in technology, television when it was first introduced was regarded as no more than a new toy, a minor innovation in the art of popular entertainment not deserving to be taken seriously. This attitude has persisted long after television has become a ubiquitous, highly influential element of our social, cultural, and intellectual environment. Most people spend a significant part of their leisure time in front of the television: it supplies most of their news of the world; it shapes their political attitudes and decisions; and it decisively affects their living styles through the goods it entices them to acquire. Yet few serious attempts have been made to analyze the essential character of this technological innovation and to evaluate what its long-term effects on society might be.

Innumerable and laborious attempts *have* been made by specialists—psychologists, sociologists, market researchers—to define and even to quantify particular aspects of the impact of television. Such investigations tend to use methods of public opinion or market research designed to produce clear-cut, measurable results on specific points: the effects of a particular advertising campaign, the public's response to a new type of packaging. When these methods have been extended to larger and more complex areas, the findings have proved more questionable and less conclusive. The multi-volume reports of British, Canadian, and American parliamentary and congressional commissions investigating matters like TV violence and pornography molder unread and unheeded on library shelves without having illuminated such vexing questions as whether sex on television increases or reduces the incidence of rape or whether violence on the screen leads to more or less violent crime in real life.

## The Medium and the Messages

Of the attempts made to evaluate the impact of television from the broadest possible point of view, none has been more daring and intriguing than that undertaken by the late Canadian critic and media scholar Marshall McLuhan, whose pronouncements are usually encapsulated in the slogan from his book *Understanding Media:* "The medium is the message."

What does this axiom mean? Essentially this: television and radio have brought about a fundamental change in the way we perceive the world; they have extended the range of our sensual apparatus by enabling us to see and hear things happening at the other end of the world. Whereas most of the information we received hitherto came to us via the printed page, in words and still pictures, we now hear our leaders discuss their political agenda and see their faces while they do so. Listening to a speech in the presence of the orator gives us a completely different feeling than does a solitary reading of the same text, when we are locked into our own private consciousness. In the spiral of historic development, McLuhan says, we have returned—on a different and higher level—to a situation similar to that of tribal societies whose members could all congregate in the center of the village to listen to their leaders, priests, or shamans. In that respect we are now members of what he calls the "global village." The age of civilization based on reading, on a written literature, is over. In our new era of oral communication, the linear, discursive mode of thought is going to be replaced, McLuhan maintains, by a primarily image-oriented type of perception and thinking.

Undoubtedly this is an insight of the utmost importance. At the same time it is sweepingly overstated in the understandable excitement of its author's prophetic fervor and, because it is so generalized, is too lofty to have had a practical impact on our everyday attitudes and practices. Hence, nothing seems to have been done to translate this important insight into any kind of concrete social action. The medium is indeed the message, but only in the widest possible sense, on a long-term secular time scale, from the perspective of a historian whose eye spans the millennia. The coming of television *has* deeply changed a culture based on the concentrated, solitary, attentive habit of reading and has largely replaced it with a new way of perceiving reality, a new mode of thought—more relaxed, diffuse, multidimensional, and immediate. This change in the structure of human perception and modes of thought will lead to fundamentally different attitudes toward the world, society, and culture. An understanding of this development on its long-term, macroscopic scale is essential. But by implying that the innumerable subsidiary influences, the multiple localized messages carried by the medium—the news, the stories of daytime serials, the product information in the commercials—are of negligible importance compared to the "basic," universal message, McLuhan discourages further thought about how to deal with the effects of television on a more mundane level.

An awareness of McLuhan's insight must underlie all attempts to adjust our ways of thinking, our institutions, and our social habits to the television age. But just as our awareness that the telephone has radically affected our lives does not diminish the importance of the details of a particular telephone call—a change in the arrival time of an expected visitor, for instance—it is not sufficient simply to accept the credo "The medium is the message" and ignore the innumerable other "messages" that are carried by television.

In the operation of any communications medium there is always a hierarchy of message conveyors. For example, in telegraphy there is the wire or wavelength, the Morse code (or some other code that might be used), the language in which the message is conveyed, and only then the explicit

*Mark* postscript to *34 Drawings for Dante's Inferno* by Robert Rauschenberg. 1964. Collection, The Museum of Modern Art, New York.

meaning of the message. On top of that, there are still a multitude of implicit messages, including the symbolic meaning and the emotional impact of the communication.

The hierarchy of messages and message conveyors in television requires a similar sort of analysis. At one end is TV's most generalized aspect, the nature of the process of communication itself. That is the end of the spectrum McLuhan is concerned with. For him the main message is: time and space have been abolished; we can all be present at the same event; our eyes and ears have immensely increased their powers; we have to see the world differently—think in a new way! At the other end we have the specific data imparted at the level of, say, a news report or commercial—an announcement that a certain make of car is now available at reduced prices. But between the most general and the most particular messages and message conveyors is an intermediate level of communication of the utmost importance, namely the "language" in which the message is conveyed (the word *language* here is used, in the vocabulary of modern linguistics, in its sense of *langue* as opposed to *parole*)—more precisely, the nature, structure, and grammar of that language.

## The Language of Television

It is my contention, the contention of this book, that we can gain considerable insight into the nature of the television medium, and a better understanding of its operation, if we recognize that the "language" in question is in fact one that has a tradition as old as civilization itself; that a great deal of thought has already been invested in the unraveling of the intricacies of its grammar and syntax; that we already possess something like a valid terminology and tested critical strategies to approach it, as well as effective tools to analyze its psychology and impact. It is, in fact, my contention that the language of television is none other than that of *drama*; that television—as indeed the cinema, with which it has much in common—is, in its essence, a *dramatic medium*; and that looking at TV from the point of view and with the analytical tools of dramatic criticism and theory might contribute to a better understanding of its nature and many aspects of its psychological, social, and cultural impact, both in the short term and on a long-term, macroscopic time scale.

On the most obvious level television is a dramatic medium simply because a large proportion of the material it transmits is in the form of traditional drama, consisting of fictional material mimetically represented by actors and employing plot, dialogue, character, gesture, costume—the whole pan-oply of dramatic means of expression. According to one of the leading statistical summaries of the television market in the United States, *The Media Book*, no less than 59 percent of the average American adult male's viewing time in 1976–77 was devoted to material in explicitly dramatic form—serials, movies, and prime-time network shows. The corresponding figure for the average American female was even higher: at least 63 percent of the time she spent watching television was devoted to shows in explicitly dramatic form. According to the 1980 edition of *The Media Book*, in the spring of 1979 American men on the average watched television for over 21 hours each week, while the average American woman's view-ing time reached just over 25 hours a week. The time devoted by the average American adult male to watching dramatic material on television thus amounts to over 12 hours per week, while the average American woman sees almost 16 hours of drama on television each week. That means that the average American adult sees the equivalent of *five to six full-length stage plays a week!*

A hundred years ago even the most assiduous theatergoer would not have seen more than one play a week over a given year, and only a small proportion of the population of the Western world lived in cities that had permanent theaters. Most people lived in areas visited only sporadically, if at all, by touring companies and thus hardly ever saw a play. Today the average American is exposed to as much drama *in a week* as the most zealous theater buff of the past century would have seen in several months!

The sheer volume of material broadcast in explicitly and traditionally dramatic form is in itself sufficient to establish television as a dramatic medium. But that, to me, is only the most obvious and superficial aspect of the matter. It is my contention in this book that whatever else it might present to its viewers, television as such displays the basic characteristics of the dramatic mode of communication—and *thought*, for drama is also a method of thinking, of experiencing the world and reasoning about it. After all, much of our thinking consists in devising scenarios for different situations and decisions—which is using drama as a form of thought.

But, one might object, drama is fiction, and much that is seen on television is real—the transmission of actual events. Well, yes and no. The dividing line between reality and art, between nature and its artistic representation, has ever been a tenuous one. When in 1917 the French avant-garde painter Marcel Duchamp submitted a urinal to be displayed in an art exhibition in New York, he drew attention to a phenomenon of basic importance: once an object, man-made or natural, is taken out of its ordinary context and put onto a pedestal or into a frame, it is made to say, "Look at me; I am here to be observed!" and immediately that object acquires some characteristics of a work of art. In its new context the urinal is seen as a form, a three-dimensional shape rather than as an object of daily use. Its significance is transformed by the act of showing it off.

The function of the stage in the theater is analogous to that of the pedestal or the frame in an art museum. If a cat walks onto the stage by accident during a performance, it automatically becomes a performer and will be perceived by the audience as having some sort of significance in the play—it may get laughs or even applause—for anything that appears on a stage proclaims that it is on display, meant to be seen, meant to fill some role or have some function within a fictional context. An ordinary chair on a stage, used in a performance of *Hamlet*, becomes an object of fiction; it plays the part of a chair in medieval, fictional Elsinore. In the same manner the man who plays Hamlet becomes the fictional prince of medieval Denmark while also remaining his real self and being observed and admired by the audience as himself, the star. And, likewise, the newscaster who reads the evening news becomes, simply by appearing in the framed square of the television screen, a performer on a stage, an actor.

The TV screen is both a frame, like Duchamp's pedestal, and a stage. Even when the news an announcer reads has been forgotten, the character he creates, his TV personality, will remain in the viewer's memory. The news changes from night to night, but the character of the newscaster persists in the public eye and the public imagination.

The information the newscaster transmits would appear to be the least fictional, least dramatized element on television, and yet most events that can be reported on the news are to some degree *staged*. Whatever reality they possess, in the sense that they actually happened, is most likely to have been filtered through various stages of a process of presentation. Moreover, the version of such events that an audience views on TV news is rarely transmitted live; it is first selectively framed, then filmed or videotaped, and finally edited in a manner that tends once more to emphasize the event's dramatic qualities. Similar considerations apply to other "real" events broadcast on television. The politician's speech and the interview or press conference with a public figure are also, inevitably, framed, stage-managed, and manipulated. The face of the great man or woman has been made up, the background chosen or designed, the clothes carefully selected, and what is televised will have been either edited on film or videotape or, if live, dramatically structured by the use of close-ups, long-shots, and reaction shots of the guest and interviewers. The final result is a dramatic performance, which moreover, filmed or videotaped, is infinitely repeatable.

This *repeatability* is a no less fundamental aspect of the theater—and all drama. Real events happen only once and are irreversible and unrepeatable; drama looks like a real event but can be repeated at will. Plays can have long runs or can be revived from a script. As most of television is recorded, most things seen on TV can be rerun. By the time a news event has been taped, edited, and shown several times, it has acquired the characteristics of a dramatic performance: it has become a dramatic artifact. Thus even the relatively rare unrehearsed events captured on TV turn into drama. Consider the televised murder of Lee Harvey Oswald by Jack Ruby. Cameras had been put into position to observe an expected event, the transfer of Oswald from police head-quarters in Dallas to the Dallas County Jail. But an unex-pected event occurred. The confusion on the screen at the instant when Jack Ruby fired point-blank into Oswald's ab-domen, and the fact that the TV viewer could hardly make out what was happening, is a memorable demonstration of the importance of planning and stage management in the filming of news events. Because Oswald's shooting was un-foreseen, it was filmed out of focus and was hardly discern-able. Nevertheless, the moment it had been recorded, the event became endlessly repeatable and now, when viewed again, can be regarded as a piece of high drama—albeit poorly produced, because unplanned.

The great event that *can* be prepared for becomes a full-scale dramatic production. The first landing of a man on the moon—one of the most spectacular of human events—was thus meticulously stage-managed for television. Cameras were installed in a manner designed to provide the best and most dramatic pictures, and the event itself unfolded in a sequence of preliminaries, explanations, and emotion-charged commentaries building to a cleverly calculated, super-dramatic climax to a grand performance when the chief as-tronaut, the star of the play, spoke his carefully prepared text. The framing of everything that is seen on television and the repeatability of most of its material inevitably turn all of television into a "show." It is no wonder that the medium is perceived overwhelmingly as an instrument of entertain-ment and a purveyor of fiction.

## A Sliding Scale of Reality

To be able to apply critical judgment to the material shown on TV, it is important, in the light of such manipulation of events, to be aware of the degree to which what appears is staged and deliberately planned. In this effort it is useful to consider the various types of television programs and arrange

Jack Ruby about to fire point-blank into Lee Harvey Oswald's abdomen. © 1963 The Dallas Morning News. Photo: Wide World Photos.

them along a spectrum: at one end will be the wholly fictional ingredients, at the other the wholly "real," least staged or stage-managed glimpses of the real world.

Let us try to consider what such a spectrum would look like, starting from the end of maximum reality: a *wholly unforeseen event* that happened to occur in the presence of a television or film camera—the bank robbery recorded by an automatic camera falls into this category, or the shots of the assassination of President Kennedy. But most of the *news reports* seen on television contain a larger amount of staging: for the arrival of an important diplomatic visitor or the departure of freed hostages, cameras have been carefully placed, the most dramatic angles chosen, and the film carefully edited to extract the maximum of dramatic effect. Demonstrations and political rallies are, by their very nature, produced dramatic events with a preordained pattern, specially

Astronaut Edwin Aldrin on the moon's surface during the Apollo II EVA, 1969. Photo: Courtesy NASA/
Ames Research Center.

designed banners and devices, and rehearsed slogans. The same is true with interviews with politicians or victims of crime and with "feature" stories about current social problems. All these items on television contain a high degree of "reality," but that reality is strongly filtered through a staging and production process.

Next on our scale would come *live sports programs*. These are also "real" in the sense that the outcome of the contest is unknown and its course wholly spontaneous. But at the same time a sports broadcast contains a considerable degree of staging: the event itself is anticipated and planned; the various cameras are carefully positioned at strategic points; during the broadcast, the director will cut cunningly from one camera to the other, from long-shot to close-up, from one end of the field to the other, from rapid "live" action to the slow-motion replay (repeatability in another form).

The *talk show*, in which real personalities are subjected to what appears to be spontaneous questioning, still contains a degree of unforeseen reality and should stand next on our spectrum. But here too we find a ritualized framework: the host figure—in most cases a popular comedian, actor, or singer with a well-defined public personality that has become his stock-in-trade—has prepared his introductory remarks as well as many of his questions, quips, and witticisms. The people being interviewed are usually show business personalities with public personae to project and, more likely than not, they have prepared and even prerehearsed much of what they say. They are, after all, judged by the public—and by the producers—on how amusing they are. If they are not sparkling and witty, they will not be asked to appear again. The talk show thus already contains a large amount of fully rehearsed dramatic material, and is in fact essentially a variety show closely related to "spectaculars" and "specials" that descend from vaudeville and the music hall tradition, old forms of popular theatrics.

Another important area of TV programming, the *game show*, combines elements of both the sports event and the talk show but should be placed nearer to the fictional end of the reality spectrum. The prescribed format of game shows

Johnny Carson as Carnac the Magnificent on "The Tonight Show." Photo: Courtesy of NBC.

is structured so that the possibility of the genuinely unrehearsed event, while still present, is greatly circumscribed. Though the contestants who compete for prizes do not know the questions in advance and the winner is not predetermined, it is quite clear that the guests are being manipulated by the master of ceremonies, the host visibly in charge—as well as by the invisible producer in the wings. The game show host is an actor following a carefully prepared part, and the contestants, assiduously screened for their dramatic potential, are displayed and moved around as actors in a ritualized framework designed to extract from them the maximum in dramatic and emotional impact.

Significantly, the mainstay of American TV and its most pervasive element—the *commercial*—has also become, more and more, a genre of drama. Although one can still occasionally see the old type of commercial, in essence a televised newspaper ad displayed to be read, most commercials are now elaborately staged minidramas, which would thus be located at the fictional end of our spectrum. That the television commercial—the lifeblood of America's entire commercial system and one of the most significant art forms of our age—has moved so completely into the field of drama underscores the fact that TV is essentially a medium of dramatic expression and communication. And this has important social and cultural consequences, as we shall see.

Before we embark on a more detailed examination of the implications of the essentially dramatic nature of TV, we must examine the basic features of drama as a method of communication and expression in order to see how TV exploits these characteristics and how we can gain control over the power of TV through our understanding of them.

Francesca Annis as Lillie Langtry in Masterpiece Theatre's "Lillie." Photo: WGBH Educational Foundation.

# 2

# Drama as Communication

DRAMA CAN BE DISCUSSED from a number of different view-
points: literary, artistic, or technological. It can also be examined simply as a technique of communication, different—
in some respects more efficient, in some less so—from other
ways in which human beings convey messages to one another. There may be messages drama can convey better than
any other form of communication, others that it may not be
able to handle well at all. What then are the main characteristics of drama, its strengths and weaknesses as a method
of communication?

### Narration vs. Drama

Let us begin with a concrete example, by comparing the
way a novelist and a director of a dramatic performance communicate the equivalent content to their respective audiences. The novelist might, for instance, introduce a new character into his story in the following manner:

> And then a young woman of remarkable beauty
> entered the room. She was tall, had honey-colored
> hair, a round face, deep blue eyes, a firm, full

mouth above a well-rounded yet energetic chin. She wore a dress of pale blue velvet, elegantly cut in a slightly old-fashioned style, with white lace trimmings. The expression on her face was serious, not to say melancholy, and yet, at times, the shadow of a mischievous smile seemed to hover around the corners of her mouth. . . .

And so on at some length. What the novelist has to communicate over a considerable period of time through the accumulation of a number of distinct items of information, the director of the dramatic performance can convey in a single moment, simply by having an actress of the desired appearance and dress enter upon the stage. Whereas the reader of the novel has to keep each item of information in his mind while the others are added one by one, line by line, to build up the complete picture, the spectator of a dramatic performance receives them as one image and with a correspondingly more immediate emotional impact. The information conveyed by the linear, discursive method of the novelist has to pass through the reader's consciousness before it can coalesce into a picture in his mind. By contrast, the spectator of a dramatic performance will get the picture at the outset, though most of the components of the impression will remain below the threshold of full consciousness.

The novelist can control the features he includes in his description and he will select them carefully. The director of the dramatic performance will try to do the same: he will select an actress whose appearance corresponds to the author's description; he will choose a dress intended to convey the qualities required by the character and the situation in which she finds herself in the scene; he will rehearse the expression with which she is to enter the room. But the actress will possess an almost infinite number of other features and characteristics that the director cannot control. Which of these features the spectator will consciously become aware of will depend on his or her own personal reaction, talent for observation, mood, and any number of other factors that are equally beyond the director's control. One spectator may detect a resemblance between the actress and his own sister; another might notice her costume and recognize the designer who created it—an item of information perhaps unknown to the director himself and one that he may never have intended to convey!

The novelist's description may also evoke subconscious associations in the reader's mind. But in the dramatic performance there are an infinite number of items of *concrete information* conveyed to the spectator at every moment. In this respect drama—which can best be defined as a mimetic reproduction of the world—mirrors the situation in our "real" lives: we are constantly confronted with people and situations we have to view, recognize, and interpret; we are compelled to select the information we need by concentrating on a few significant features and rejecting the bulk of data that continuously bombard our senses. Nevertheless there is an essential difference between a dramatic performance and the world of "reality": reality occurs spontaneously and unrepeatably, whereas the dramatic performance has been deliberately engineered to produce in us an intended emotional and intellectual response. Although drama necessarily shares many of the features of reality, it is of course only a simulation of reality and is, above all, simplified, compressed, reordered, manipulated, reversible, and repeatable.

There is a commonplace of dramatic production that in the course of rehearsals, during the endless discussions between the director, designer, writer, and cast concerning the psychology of the characters and their appearance and environment, someone invariably will interject that such discussion is futile because the audience will not notice these fine points of detail. To which, equally invariably, the director will respond that though the audience may not notice such details consciously, subliminally they will take them in and their responses will be affected. And this is undoubtedly true. What is also true, however, is that many things that were not discussed and not intended will affect as strongly the conscious or unconscious reaction of individuals in the audience, each of whom will have to come to terms with what he or she has seen and heard.

# Decoding Drama

Because the communication in drama occurs not in a linear sequence but in tightly bundled clusters of data that bombard the senses, the spectator's task of decoding a dramatic performance is very different from the reader's task of decoding a novel. To return to our initial example: the entrance of the beautiful woman on the stage will produce an immediate emotional effect (provided, that is, that the director has skillfully focused the attention of the audience upon that entrance). But few members of the audience will be able to say subsequently why they found the woman beautiful: whether it was the shadow of the mischievous smile that played upon her otherwise melancholy countenance or the lace trimmings on her well-cut dress or her deep blue eyes—if indeed they *did* find her beautiful, which some may not have. Those who did may merely remember a sense of mystery and elegance. Some may, either during the performance or afterward, try to analyze the beauty of the woman as they remember particular features in detail. But almost certainly the features they call to mind will be different from those the novelist used to build his picture. And most of the audience will remain unaware of all these distinct details and their interaction.

But, it may be objected, our example concerns a purely visual image, the *appearance* of a character on stage before that character has uttered a single word. Is not drama, like the novel, primarily made up of words and therefore subject to the same mechanisms of expression and understanding as any other verbal form of communication, whether it be a novel, a newspaper dispatch, or a scientific treatise?

Drama does contain an element of the linear and abstract, but everything that is said on the stage emerges from human beings who are perceived primarily as images and, accordingly, what they say is merely a secondary function of those images. The verbal element will of necessity either reinforce or contradict the primary message of the image to which it is subordinate. If, say, Iago assures Othello of his affection, but has an expression of burning hatred in his eyes, the verbal element will clearly be devalued. It is what the characters do, not what they say, that matters in drama. In the famous final scene of Samuel Beckett's *Waiting for Godot* one of the two weary men says "Let's go" but the stage direction—and the action of the two characters—is what matters: "They do not move." In either case the primacy of the visual, situational, concrete element—the image—over the abstract content of the verbal element is inescapable.

It is a cliché of the theater that a good director could fascinate an audience by staging a reading of the telephone directory: such a director would invent intriguing images that would make the audience forget that the words they hear are only a list of names. But no one who needed a number from the phone book would find it expedient to seek it in a dramatic performance. There follows from this a very simple but critical insight: drama is not the most effective way to communicate abstract or purely verbal content or information. If the content is primarily abstract or verbal, it can better be conveyed by silent reading or by recitation, without the full spectrum of means available to stage or screen.

In a dramatic performance on a stage or on a television or movie screen the number of sign systems (i.e., systems of significance) involved is extraordinary. The full range of verbal language (on which the novelist must rely) and the full gamut of voice expression (which so powerfully augments whatever is read on the radio) are enhanced by a vast array of other sign systems. Not only does the appearance of the actor's face and body convey an immense amount of information, but his gestures and movements are signs as well in a complex system of body language. Costumes form another complete sign system, that of dress and its meanings. To this is added the visual sign system of the setting—whether painted or three-dimensional, as on the stage, or photographically conveyed, as on the screen—as well as the elaborate system of significances contained in props: the furniture of a room or the architecture of a building. There is also the system of signs in the lighting plot and that in the musical background that underlies most movies and many television shows. Still another sign system in both movies and television is the variation of shots (long, medium, close) and their montage—the juxtaposition of long-shots to close-ups and the cutting from one scene or shot to another. It is impossible to assign each of these sign systems a rigidly maintained rank on a ladder of rising priorities, but one point should be evident: *in drama the complex, multilayered image predominates over the spoken word.*

## Aspects of Personality

Drama is about people in social interaction; the primary interest of the spectator of drama is attached to the personalities involved, their appearance and character, their effects on each other. The linguistic element, insofar as it is concerned with the transmission of abstract ideas, may often come very far down our ladder, after gesture and movement, after costume, even after the impact of the setting.

In drama, at any given moment, the spectator receives a complex of information that coalesces into a general impression, an *image* with an emotional impact, which consists of numerous elements that will remain below the threshold of consciousness but will always be focused upon a human personality, a character. The brightness of the sunshine, the airiness of the lovely buildings on the square, the lively rhythm of the background music, the vivid colors of the costume the actor wears, the springiness of his steps all contribute to the spectator's impression that the young lover he sees in front of him is supremely happy, but few in the audience will be aware of the many elements of information that come together to produce this impression. Drama is always action; its action is always that of human beings. In drama we experience the world through personality.

When we are presented with abstract ideas on the printed page, we may overlook or forget that they are the product of the thought of the individual who has written the text; we may thus receive these ideas as abstract truths. But in drama what we hear is always spoken by a specific individual and has value only as his or her own pronouncement. When we see *Hamlet*, we may accept the words of Hamlet himself or

Polonius or Horatio as containing abstract moral or philosophical truths or insights, or we may not. Nothing in the play constrains us to believe the words spoken represent more than the thoughts of the characters—thoughts influenced by their personalities and motives. We are merely informed what this or that character is saying, not necessarily even whether he himself believes what he is saying or whether he is trying to deceive his interlocutor.

Whenever attempts have been made to introduce abstraction into drama—as in morality plays of the late Middle Ages and early Renaissance in which virtues and vices appeared as emblematic figures: Faith, Good Works, Gluttony, Lechery—the figures of these abstractions inevitably turned into individualized characters. And, paradoxically, the vices, by appearing more human, usually more effectively captured the sympathy of their audiences. In the abstract, Faith or Chastity may have been preferable characteristics; on the stage, individualized and humanized, Avarice or Lechery were easier to identify with, more amusing, and therefore more attractive. Allegorical characters have by no means disappeared. They thrive in our time in television commercials, as exemplified, say, by the demons of dirt and grime infesting clogged drains.

The element of personality in drama appears in a highly complex form. When we see Olivier or Gielgud as Hamlet we are interested and involved not only in the fictitious character of Hamlet, but also in the real personality of Laurence Olivier or John Gielgud. The two, character and actor, are fused almost inextricably, so that it is difficult to say which it is that mainly attracts or interests us. Yet it *is* possible to say that we like Olivier's Hamlet better than Gielgud's, or even that we were fascinated by Gielgud's but utterly bored by X's portrayal.

### Literature and Drama

At the same time, we know that the character of Hamlet himself as he exists in Shakespeare's play is one that will always be intriguing. This consideration highlights another essential point about the nature of drama as a method of communication: plays that are merely read are literature, and they adhere to the same principles of perception as the novel. If we read *Hamlet* the process of communication we experience is the same as that when we read *War and Peace*. The difference is merely that the descriptive passages in the play—the stage directions—are shorter and the dialogue passages more numerous than in the novel. But in reading *Hamlet* we are, as in reading *War and Peace*, transforming the signs on the page, word by word, line by line, into mental images that coalesce into something like the equivalent of a performance. Seeing a play performed reverses that process and is—with respect to the act of communication that is taking place—totally different.

Those exceptional dramatic texts that have achieved over time the status of literature provide powerful evidence of the essential difference between literature and drama as methods of communication. In performance a dramatic text can convey very different meanings each time it is presented. A performance of *Hamlet*, to stick with our example, is totally different today from a performance of the same text a hundred, two hundred, or three hundred years ago. Not only have the words themselves been uttered in different styles of pronunciation and expressiveness from century to century, not only have costumes and the spatial and visual configuration of the stage changed but, because of the many additional sign systems superimposed in performance upon the basic blueprint of the written text, different sorts of communication are taking place at each performance and very different meanings are being conveyed.

There is of course an essential *core* to such a play: the basic structure of its plot, the interaction of its characters, and the imagery contained in the language. But apart from the obvious differences in acting style, stage technology, and directing, there are also fundamental differences between a performance, say, for Elizabethans who believed in the physical existence of ghosts and one for an audience today that will regard the play's ghost as, at best, a metaphor for Hamlet's subconscious fears or suspicions. The fundamental char-

Laurence Olivier as Hamlet with Basil Sydney as Claudius in *Hamlet*. Photo: National Film Archive/Stills Library, London.

acteristic of a play-text that remains performable over a period of centuries is that it lends itself—thanks to the durability of the language and depth of the attitudes intrinsic to it—to the production of an almost infinite number of different styles, evoking as many different meanings. A look at the repertoire of theaters throughout the world shows how relatively rare texts of this kind actually are.

Applying these considerations from the history of classical stage drama to the proliferation of drama today in the mass media, we can immediately sense their force. How much of the fictionalized drama seen every day on commercial television could bear translation into written texts and come to be regarded as literature by generations hence? Indeed, how many scripts of even highly successful movie "classics" could be considered literature? Of course, in movies the dramatic performance and the text have been inextricably fused by the process of mechanical recording. Thus we can now look back on some eighty years of such recorded performances. Even after so relatively short a lapse of time, however, it is clear that few of even the most outstanding movies (such as the greatest Garbo, Dietrich, D.W. Griffith, Chaplin, or Marx Brothers films) survive the passage of the years without a profound modification of their impact and meaning. When we view an old movie today, for example, elements such as the fashions of the period, commonplace and hardly noticed at the time, become valuable items of historical interest and may overshadow either the plot or the performance of the principal actors, which were, originally, major features of the film. The meaning of the text itself may also change over time: it can become a period piece as language evolves and as the concepts and conditions it describes change.

What all these considerations highlight once again is that a performance, whether live (and thus subject to variation in each presentation) or mechanically recorded (and thus fixed once and for all), will carry a richer, more complex package of meaning-producing systems than will the written word alone. This multilayered dramatic package will produce an emotional impact the elements of which remain largely subliminal. And the abstract, purely intellectual content of a performed dramatic work will tend to be subordinate to its emotional impact, which is principally the outcome of the interaction of characters, human personalities.

Like the stage and the cinema screen, television deals primarily in images—not only the explicitly dramatic programs broadcast but *all* of television. It is impossible merely to transmit a text on TV unless it is being shown as a silent caption (in which case it is really a means of distributing the printed word). The moment an announcement is read by a speaker on camera a multitude of dramatic sign systems are unleashed. The intention may be only to let us know that "today is Wednesday the twenty-third of May," but we are being informed as well that these words are spoken by a good-looking male of about thirty-five years of age with a blond moustache, that the studio in which he is sitting has a window with a view of midtown Manhattan, that the young man is wearing a tie with blue stripes, that he has a wedding band on his left hand and a wart on his right cheek. We are getting one line of information from the text he is speaking, but at the same time a flood of data is being released about him and his environment. Whether he intends it or not, he has become a *character* in the primary dramatic sense.

## Dramatis Personae

The frame of the television screen turns everything that happens on it into a stage and everything that is seen or heard upon it into a sign. What is more important, everything that takes place upon that stage has an emotional impact. For instance, we probably respond to the young man announcing the date either favorably or unfavorably. The emotional charge that powers our response in this case may be mild or even subconscious. But in the long run our attitude toward him or one of his rivals may determine which station we select when we watch the news. An awareness of this fact will lie behind the decision of the network's or station's management when it chooses its anchors. It will also shape the anchors' decisions about how to dress and how to conduct themselves, in other words, about what kind of character they will try to present to the viewers.

In a television game show the contestant's answer to a question is less important than his reaction to his success or failure in finding the proper answer—his visible distress if he has failed, his jumping for joy if he has succeeded. In the political interview, however important the personality being questioned may be, however momentous the topics upon which he is speaking, our real interest springs from watching his or her reaction to the sharp searching and provocative questioning to which he or she is being subjected. We are not primarily getting facts; we are getting drama, which is to say we are getting information about the character we are watching rather than about the subject under discussion.

As a method of communication, therefore, drama is highly effective in conveying *human character*, and much less effective

*Desi Arnaz and Lucille Ball in a breakfast scene from "I Love Lucy." Photo: Culver Pictures.*

in communicating ideas or abstract thought, simply because in drama every abstract idea has to be incarnated as the utterance of an individual and that individual tends to occupy the foreground and to overpower, at least to some degree, the impact of the ideas he or she is voicing. Moreover, as our reactions to individuals are differentiated by our tastes, memories, and fantasies, ideas communicated via television tend to be judged in the light of our reaction to the personalities conveying them. Whether we respond favorably or unfavorably to the multitude of subliminal signals that make up the total impact of such personalities will largely determine whether we accept or reject the ideas they purvey—insofar as we take these ideas in at all.

Since actors are the pivotal point, the central and sole essential ingredient of drama, the effectiveness of television performers of all kinds will derive from their ability to project personality, in other words, from their talent as actors. In this respect it is interesting to note how miserably most inexperienced speakers appear on television, speakers such as one occasionally sees in the spots the stations provide for reply to their own editorial opinions. The expressionless faces of the people on these spots as they tonelessly read a prepared text points up the demands on the usual television performer, to be not only a professional but a professional with acting talent. What these untrained speakers have to say rarely has any impact on the viewers. On television a message delivered by a person without acting talent is hardly noticed at all.

The situation is entirely different when television catches actual participants in news events at moments of high emotion: the relatives of a murder victim, hostages who have been released, eyewitnesses to an accident, and so on. The emotional intensity of the situation—its drama—turns such neophytes into effective performers able to project an intense state of mind and genuine passion. The participants in game shows are in a similarly excited emotional state, which tends to transform them too into effective actors (though they have, in addition, been carefully pretested for their natural acting ability, attractiveness, or quirkiness of character).

The ability of TV to transmit personality is, undoubtedly, the secret of its immense power. For human beings are insatiable in their interest about other human beings. Once, when traveling through a remote region of then-colonial East Africa and seeing the villages of grass huts without shops or electricity or roads or any other amenities, I asked an African friend what the local people did during the long dark hours after nightfall, which at the equator comes early the whole year round. Without hesitation my friend replied, "They gossip. They tell each other about the love affairs and sicknesses of their neighbors." Indeed this seems to me one of the basic human drives. Next to the satisfaction of the drives for food, shelter, and procreation, the satisfaction of the drive to gossip about the experiences of others must be one of the central concerns of all human existence. It is the source of all fiction and storytelling, and the source too of drama. Hearing about what has happened to other people, how they have coped with crises in their lives, is of the utmost importance to the survival of the individual and of the species; it is part of an endless learning process.

Herein lies the source of humanity's insatiable craving for stories: all fiction is ultimately gossip. Television, with its unending stream of characters conveyed dramatically (whether fictional or "real"), is the most perfect mechanized conveyor of that gossip. Being essentially dramatic rather than discursive in nature, moreover, television satisfies this craving in a uniquely effective manner; it not only retells stories *about* other people, it actually transports these other people into our own living rooms. The attraction of gossip, of course, contains at its root one of the most powerful human impulses. Our interest in other people contains of necessity a strong erotic element. It is this which constitutes one of the basic characteristics and magnetic powers of drama: drama is basically *erotic*. Actors give the spectators who watch them a great deal of pleasure simply by being interesting, memorable, or beautiful physical specimens of humanity. Quite apart from their artistic and intellectual accomplishments, actors are people who, for money, exhibit their physical presence to the public. We all know that great stars derive their special magnetism from sex appeal. But what applies to the big stars contributes as well to the attractiveness and success of the lesser lights. In a sense all actors are exhibitionists: they enjoy being seen, being found appealing and worth looking at. Conversely audiences of drama are also, in a certain sense, voyeurs.

Though this is true of all drama, it is especially true of television. Television is the most voyeuristic of all communication media, not only because it provides more material in an unending stream of images and in the form most universally accessible to the totality of the population, but also because it is the most intimate of the dramatic media. In the theater the actors are relatively remote from the audience, and the dramatic occasion is public. In the cinema, also a public occasion gathering a large audience into a single room, the actors are nearer to the spectators than in the theater, but in close-ups they are larger than life. Television is seen at a close range and in a more private context. The close-up of

"We're at the home of Jim and Mindy Marks, who are about to discover
that their utility bill has gone sky-high. Let's watch."

the television performer is on a scale that most nearly approximates direct human contact.

## The Daydream Machine

The appeal of television is, at the most basic level, an erotic appeal. TV brings other human beings into close proximity for detailed inspection. The people we view in close-ups on the television screen appear to be as near to us as our sexual partners during an embrace. And yet they are glimpsed behind a glass screen, through a window that cannot be opened. The television screen is a stage, a frame for the display of images, but though so near, the world it brings to us is also beyond our reach, a world of inaccessible phantoms. The world it shows us on its stage, behind that window through which we can see but cannot grasp or touch, is essentially a world of fantasy.

Thus television is closely akin to the daydream. The essential feature of daydreams is that they are outside our conscious control. Their charm lies precisely in the spontaneous images they flash before our mind's eye, to which we surrender passively and with pleasure. Television images are received in this same way. Hollywood earned for the movie industry the tag "dream factory" in its early years of mass-entertainment production; in a similar way the television industry has engineered a product that can be called the "daydream machine," for TV brings an uninterrupted procession of collective daydreams, collective fantasies, into our homes. It is this essential characteristic of television that accounts for the blurring of the distinction between fact and fiction, the real world and fantasy, on the screen.

Our daydreams, after all, also concern themselves with the real world; through them we may even reach important decisions, evolve plans, and devise strategies for future conduct. Daydreams nevertheless remain fantasies; they are experienced as intuitions to which we surrender passively rather than as processes of consciously directed, inductive reasoning. Even the most "real" features of television, such as the news, contain the element of fantasy, and of erotic fantasy at that. There is the appeal of the anchorman or anchorwoman and of the reporters, the appeal of the political personalities and other subjects of news broadcasts—hostages, beauty queens, criminals, and victims of crime. And there is the sensationalistic, even sadomasochistic, appeal of the scenes of violence, war, and disaster that make up so much of the material presented on TV news: demonstrators being beaten by police; prisoners being executed in a war or revolution; the smoldering debris left in the aftermath of a plane crash. The undoubted element of "reality" contained in the news is thus, by being broadcast on television, automatically transmuted into the stuff of fantasy and daydream—drama—into a story told in images laden with emotional overtones and sometimes hardly distinguishable from fiction.

All drama depends on that "suspension of disbelief" that will make us, for a brief time, accept the characters we see on the stage as real human beings so that we can identify with them to experience their joys and their sorrows, the whole range of their emotions. Television protracts the suspension of disbelief. What distinguishes TV from the theater and the cinema is sheer quantity of material: the continuousness of TV and the vast amount of material it spews forth enlarge and intensify the traditional characteristics of the other dramatic media so immensely that the increased *quantity* of material broadcast on TV becomes a new *qualitative* characteristic. We may have believed, for the span of three hours, that Hamlet was a real person, but then we are left to reflect on his character with detachment and analytical insight. The character in the soap opera, on the other hand, is with us almost every day over a period of years and becomes so familiar that detached reflection is inhibited or never occurs at all. Disbelief may become permanently suspended.

It is the constant presence of this alternative world that is both real and fictional—a fantasy yet an immensely real factor in the lives of whole populations—that makes the explosion of the dramatic form of communication on television such a revolutionary development.

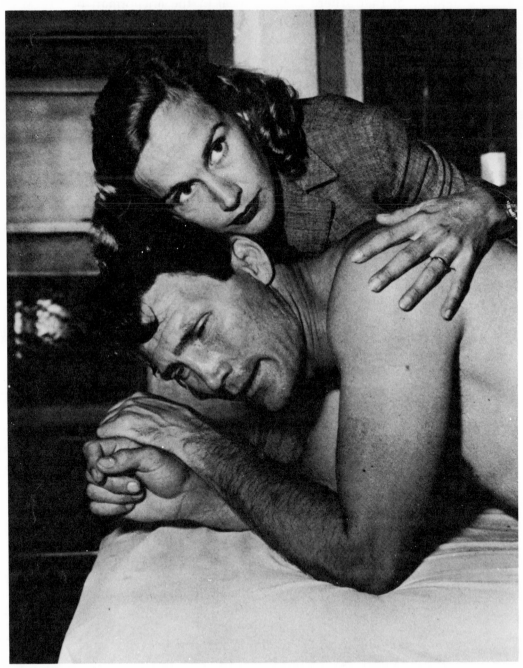

Serious drama did have a place on American TV in the 1950s: Jack Palance and Kim Hunter in Rod Serling's "Requiem for a Heavyweight" on "Playhouse 90."

# 3

# Fiction into Reality

TELEVISION, LIKE THE CINEMA, was originally regarded as no more than a convenient way to transmit existing stage plays to larger and larger masses of spectators. The BBC's television service, the first in the world to start regular operation, as early as 1936 broadcast from its studios live performances of stage plays. To simulate the ambience of the theater there were even ten-minute intervals between the acts during which the screen remained blank or was filled with a neutral image of a running brook. A shrill bell sounded shortly before the play was to be resumed to recall members of the audience from their cups of tea and visits to the lavatory. This of course was a time when television was so rare that a broadcast of a play still partook of a prime characteristic of the live theater—indeed one of its principal attractions: a sense of occasion. As TV became ever more ubiquitous, continuous, and commonplace, that sense of occasion inevitably disappeared. It is now taken almost completely for granted that whenever the television set is turned on in the course of an evening, a stream of dramatic fiction will pour forth. In that stream the presentation of stage plays, whether classical or contemporary, is becoming an ever rarer event.

In the early years of American TV not only were stage plays more frequently broadcast than today, but serious playwrights like Paddy Chayefsky and Rod Serling began to write plays for TV that could stand on their own, referred to in the professional jargon as "single plays" (to distinguish them from self-contained episodes of series and ongoing serials with their continuous story lines). This phenomenon has now practically disappeared in the United States. In other parts of the world where television is not as highly commercialized as in the U.S., TV continues to provide room for serious drama that can claim the status of a work of dramatic art. Yet even in countries like Britain, France, Germany, and Italy, where such drama still is broadcast, it is fighting a stubborn rearguard action.

Why should this be the case? It is, precisely, connected with the disappearance of that sense of occasion which is so important an ingredient of the psychological impact of the live theater and even, though to a lesser degree, of a visit to the movies. The principal feature that distinguishes television from these two other dramatic media is TV's unending flow and the fact that, because of that unending flow, anyone can at any time turn on the TV and receive its material, as one does water flowing from the tap.

In all aesthetics the psychology of the audience of a work of art must be taken into account: for example, a visitor to a museum will view a painting hanging there differently than will the owner of an original who can see the painting every day in his own home. The relative rarity of a visit to the theater, the ritual of being taken to one's seat, of opening the program all help to create a receptive state of mind in the spectator, a degree of expectation that will make him more inclined to watch the play with attentiveness, respect, and a willingness to become immersed in it. By comparison, a visit to the movie theater is less conducive to such a state of mind: here the ritual buying of popcorn, the informality in finding a seat, the previews for coming attractions that precede the main feature turn the event into a far more casual experience.

Nevertheless, the visit to the theater or the movies is still the outcome of a deliberate act, a conscious decision to go and see a certain play or film. The abundance of material on television, with its several channels of continuous programming, makes it extremely difficult to attract the attention of viewers to a specific single item. The very existence of the relatively few, heavily advertised "specials" underscores this point. Clearly it is quite impossible to make every program broadcast on television a "special event," an occasion with a *sense* of occasion, to construct a whole schedule of programs each of which could claim individual attention because of a special, unique identity. How then is order to be imposed on the amorphous mass of material that pours forth from the television set in a barely differentiated stream?

## Order out of Chaos

The answer to that problem is regularity, structure, habit-forming programs; in other words, series—regularly recurring shows. Series have a twofold advantage. To the viewer they provide a mixture of familiarity—the freedom from the need to make an intellectual effort, to think oneself into each new episode—and novelty: the recurring characters who will have become as familiar as members of one's own family will, each week, appear in new and different situations and circumstances. Each week's episode will have this same mixture, but with a slightly different flavor. In short, the series provides the viewer with a sense of security, a structure that allows him to find his way through the chaos. The fact that most programs start at the hour or half hour makes it easy for the viewer to enter the stream with a minimum of frustration. And the knowledge that a certain series will appear every Tuesday evening at 8:00 P.M. allows him to plan not to miss a favorite item. To the TV programmer the advantage of the series is even greater: he or she, after all, has to fill innumerable spots, day in and day out, week after week, ad infinitum. The producer of a stage play or a film will work on his project for a time, see it through its opening, and then, if it is a success, sit back, relax, and plan his next project. By contrast, the TV program planner's labors can never stop. To handcraft each of the endless TV spots that he must fill would be quite out of the question.

The sheer volume of the output of the medium *compels* its

producers to resort to mass production methods. The hand-crafted creation must be replaced by the products of an assembly line. Thus the logic of the medium imposes upon itself the structure of the regularly recurring item. The series enables the planner to place the same item on his schedule on any particular evening at 8:00 P.M., to be followed by another regular title at 9:00 P.M. and another at 10:00 P.M. and so on throughout the week, month, and quarter—the thirteen-week period that is the basic unit of the television planning process. Hence television program planning is basically planning in units of thirteen-week series, in addition to items that recur every weekday—soap operas and news broadcasts—and are thus even more easily planned.

This "strip planning" does allow individualized items to be accommodated, provided they can be brought under a convenient overall title that can turn these heterogeneous programs into some semblance of a regularly recurring series. That is why, for example, serializations of classical novels, British soap operas like "Upstairs, Downstairs," and dramatized detective novels are marketed on American television as "Masterpiece Theatre," a title that is as silly as it is misleading and that merely serves the purpose of homogenizing all this heterogeneous material into the semblance of a genuine series. Similarly old movies can be marketed as a pseudoseries by calling the weekly spot "The Monday Night Movie" or "The Big Show." There is nothing wrong with such a practice: it brings order into the amorphous chaos of the relentless stream of programs.

The genuine series—a sequence of programs conceived as a self-contained whole and specially designed for that purpose—is, in many ways, more satisfying to the viewer. The series is usually centered around a group of recurring characters in a recurring environment (police station, hospital, family home, newspaper office, etc.) who are presented in different circumstances and adventures each of which will form a self-contained whole. Alternatively, in the soap-opera type of structure, different strands of ongoing story lines run parallel for very long periods. A third, less frequent type in American television is what is called in British television jargon the "serial," in American parlance the "mini-series": a story told from beginning to end in a limited number of episodes each of which continues the events of the previous one. This is the form in which novels can be turned into series (*Roots, Shogun,* and classics like *The Golden Bowl* and *The Scarlet Letter*).

The series provides the program planner with an additional and important advantage over traditional drama. Every self-contained piece of traditional drama must first introduce its characters and their circumstances; it must have what is called an "exposition." However skillfully this is handled by the author and director, the exposition does demand a special kind of concentration from the audience, and it also takes a certain amount of time. In a series with recurring characters, that time can be used for other purposes because the characters are assumed to be known to the audience already. The exposition merely has to deal with the special circumstances of the particular episode. The concentration required is thus reduced, and more action can be accommodated in the restricted time allotment. Movies made for TV require a full exposition, but they are longer than the typical series episode and tend also to command a greater degree of studio attention than the episodes that come off a production line with stereotyped settings and low production budgets.

The production process involved in the creation of a series episode has its own built-in logic, which sets off the bulk of dramatized TV material from all traditional drama. Even less than the cinema feature film will this type of drama be the individual creation of a single imagination, the expression of one person's view of the world. A series episode is an industrial product the form and content of which are dictated precisely by the conditions of mass-production technology and economics.

Before production begins the product is pretested and perfected on a prototype, the *pilot program.* Immense ingenuity and effort go into the pilot. Many early attempts will be discarded, and if the tests on sample audiences prove inconclusive, the whole project may be abandoned even though large sums of money have already been spent. Once

Blackthorne (Richard Chamberlain), Lady Mariko (Yoko Shimada), and Lord Toranaga (Toshiro Mifune) in the TV mini-series adaptation of James Clavell's *Shogun*. Photo: Courtesy of NBC.

the pilot has passed its testing, the leading actors have found favor, and market research has established its potential, the pilot becomes the pattern on which all future episodes are modeled. This pattern will involve both the use of recurring settings (to save construction costs) and recurring plot elements, such as the final chase in most detective or police series—which, apart from being unfailingly suspenseful, has the advantage of being of variable length, thereby allowing the exact timing of the episode to be attained simply by trimming or expanding the chase sequence.

Once all these matters have been settled the series can be summed up in a *format*, which includes the characterization of the principal characters, the setting, and the plot structure. This format can then be distributed among the script writers who will create the individual episodes. To avoid monotony the producers will plan the series with the greatest possible variation within the preestablished pattern. Each writer will be given instructions as to the subject matter, locale, and desired mood of the episode he is to do: a heavily dramatic episode to be followed by a more lighthearted one, a sexy episode by one with a moralistic overtone, etc.

The soap operas that appear each weekday afternoon represent only a slight variation of the evening series pattern, in that their several different story lines run concurrently over many episodes. Because soap operas are seen daily, their characters are even more familiar than those on the evening series and the stories can be strung out over many weeks and months. The structural pattern dictates that a number of novelettelike plots run parallel, held together primarily by the locale—a hospital, a small town—which permits the producers to confine the action within a strictly limited number of mainly indoor settings.

## Recurring Characters in a Fictional World

Whether we look at self-contained weekly or ongoing daily episodes, the recurring characters in this type of dramatized fiction remain constant and become ever more familiar to their audiences. They are experienced by viewers in a curious manner that amounts to a kind of split consciousness. This is a phenomenon of considerable interest: though members of the audience know that the TV characters are fictitious, they also react to their experiences on the screen as though they were real. An actress portraying a character who, for example, becomes pregnant in a soap opera will receive gifts of baby clothes from viewers who know that the pregnancy is fictional. And when actors or actresses who play well-known characters on the screen make public appearances, people often treat them as if they were the characters they portray.

But these are only the outward signs of a phenomenon that has roots at a deeper level. Recurring characters often *are* more real than most people the viewers know, simply because they know these characters better than they do most of their real acquaintances. After all, the viewers have been present at the most intimate, emotion-charged moments in these characters' lives, have partaken in their love affairs, family mix-ups, and life-and-death adventures. Viewers, over a period of months or even years, have identified with these characters and have vicariously lived their lives.

In this sense, too, the quantitative aspect of the drama explosion has created an entirely new type and quality of human experience. Admittedly, ongoing characters who appear in more than one play have been a feature of drama throughout the ages: think of the stereotyped harlequins, pantalones, dottores, and capitanos of the commedia dell'arte, or indeed of the Little Tramp created by Charlie Chaplin, the stone-faced sufferer of Buster Keaton, or the Jack Sprat duo of Laurel and Hardy. Such ongoing fictitious personalities, however, were not only a relative rarity, they were seen far less frequently by the majority of their audiences than their TV counterparts today. There has sprung up with TV a whole population of archetypal figures who appear daily or weekly and who can become familiar, intimately known, easily absorbed into the fantasy life and consciousness of millions of individuals.

Fictitious figures who become more real than real people, who become archetypes of conduct, are a commonplace of human culture: the gods and heroes of ancient myth and legend are precisely such figures. So are the heroes of present-day TV, with the important difference that they are infinitely more visible and accessible than any of the great mythical heroes could ever be, because they are living presences in our homes. But, one may ask, were not Odysseus, Haroun-al-Rashid, and Till Eulenspiegel, Achilles, Siegfried, King Arthur, Lancelot, and Guinevere the outcrop of the "collective unconscious"—the collective strivings and longings, fears and ambitions of tribes and nations, the deep roots of great cultures—whereas Lucy, Kojak, Archie Bunker, and the Fonz exist mainly to maximize audiences for commercials and are thus the calculated and contrived products of hard-nosed businessmen out to make a profit? How can they be compared to gods and heroes of ancient myth and legend?

Though it may well be true that our present-day archetypal heroes cut pale figures when set side by side with those of earlier cultures, the *genesis* of today's archetypes is by no means as different as it might appear at first glance. The archetypal heroes of earlier cultures arose in response to the psychological needs of those cultures—their values, preoccupations, and tastes. Our present-day archetypes may indeed be the product of hardheaded calculations of producers looking to make a profit, but these producers themselves are in many ways ordinary people with ordinary tastes who have reached positions from which they are able to impose their ideas of what is appealing, probably because their taste agrees with that of the majority of people. The conscious—and even more so the subconscious—minds of these individuals are very likely to be particularly representative of the collective unconscious of the masses.

Moreover, long-running series and soap operas are more than merely the outcrop of the imagination of their originators. The longer the series run, the more accurately ratings and public opinion research establish the relative popularity of characters and story-line patterns. From my own experience at BBC Radio Drama with several long-running radio soap operas, I know to what an extent the audience actually dictates the creation of these archetypes. A marginal character, introduced as a filler or because an out-of-work actor needed temporary employment, will suddenly appear on top of the popularity polls among all the characters and will, accordingly, be pushed to the foreground; a tangential episode will prove so popular that it will not only be expanded but will become the model for a more elaborate version of the same problem or situation.

The pantheon of archetypal characters in ever-recurring situations on present-day American television does, I believe, accurately reflect the collective psyche, the collective fears and aspirations, neuroses and nightmares of the average American, as distinct from the factual reality of the state of the nation. Does not the prominence of hospitals and disease in story lines indicate a national preoccupation with health, even a certain hypochondria? Do not the sex kittens of the evening series accurately represent current ideals of beauty? Are not the mix-ups and grotesqueries of family situation comedies an accurate, if exaggerated, scenario of the embarrassments and triumphs of family life, real or fantasized? These programs may present caricatures of real situations, but, like all good caricature and all myth, they merely intensify and enlarge the true features of the daydreams from which they spring. These then are the collective daydreams of this culture. And daydreams are no less significant or important for being exaggerated or intensified representations of real situations or the extreme reflections of fears, anxieties, aspirations, and wishes, real or imaginary.

The myths and archetypes of a civilization are not only an outcrop of the collective unconscious of its members; they also, in a characteristic feedback process, mold and affect their longings, patterns of behavior, and attitudes. To ask which comes first, the *expression* of subconscious wishes and ideas mirrored in these archetypes or the *effect* of these archetypes on the patterns of behavior and habits of thought of the same individuals, would be as futile as to ask which comes first, the chicken or the egg. The feedback process is one of infinite complexity: social, economic, and cultural developments create needs that find expression in the utterances of certain opinion-forming individuals; these expressions find an echo, a confirmation, in the reaction of other individuals who may have been slower to respond to the same set of circumstances. Multiplied on the mass medium of television as well as by other means, these attitudes then reinforce the initial reaction of still other individuals and gradually mold the behavior of the masses. The process is a dynamic one. Whether or not it would be possible to exercise more conscious control over this process remains open to question. But, at least, an awareness of its existence and some insight into its workings are desirable.

## Mythic Cycles

What, then, are some of the main themes of this mythical or quasi-mythical universe? For a considerable time television was dominated by the "Western" myth, one of the basic myths of our civilization in the last half of the nineteenth century and in most of the twentieth—and not only in America. Generations of European as well as American children have been brought up on Western films and stories. The theme of the Western cycle of stories is the spread of European civilization to a new part of the world, the conquest of nature and the native inhabitants in that new world, and, in a second phase, the gradual establishment of law and order after the conquest. The Western myth is analogous to the Trojan war cycle dealing with the conquest of Asia Minor by the Greeks, which found its best (though by no means only) crystallization in the Homeric poems. Though the Western myth remains in evidence on television today, it has now lost its dominant position to other cycles: the spy cycle and the police cycle most especially, each with endless variations and subtypes—with the policemen sometimes officers of the law, sometimes private detectives; the spies official, unofficial, or sometimes even free-lance. The series centering on lawyers, forensic scientists, or insurance investigators are variations of the same pattern. What they all have in common is the Manichaean view that history, politics, and law enforcement are aspects of an endless struggle between purely good and purely evil forces. They offer reassurance through the inevitable victory of good over evil, but these series also reflect a more or less suppressed delight in crime and violence for its own sake.

Science fiction and space adventures are more recent additions to the mythical universe of TV. Here the escape into fantasies of omnipotence and miraculous technology provides release from the increasing awareness of impotence in an era of political decline and economic crisis. The introduction of robots or bionically enhanced types of ordinary humans similarly reflects a desire to escape from feelings of inadequacy, physical or intellectual.

Then there is the continuous stream of family myth as portrayed in domestic situation comedies. Here the embarrassments of family life are endlessly rehearsed and varied, as are the tribulations of the work place—office, factory, or store. What is remarkable is the wide variety of milieus portrayed: the locale is in fact often the starting point for the whole series ("How about setting it in a restaurant, a night club, a junk shop?"—*any* distinctive location—seems to be the basic premise). At the same time the kinds of characters and the predicaments they experience are practically uniform: timid males pursued by predatory females, the arrival of uninvited guests, and other embarrassing situations form the surprisingly restricted staple of these comedies. Their variation lies mainly in the attractiveness or absurdity of the individual characters. "How is this impossible misfit going to react to situations we all know?" or "How is that cute little lady going to cope?" are the kind of terms in which these dramas are set—a further confirmation of the importance of *character* in drama.

In the soap-opera cycle it is health and the hospital world that often forms a principal interest, though adultery, the breakdown of marriage, teenage pregnancy, racial tensions, the problems of career women, class prejudices, and a hundred other topical or eternal human concerns are also staples of the genre.

Interestingly, the large number of characters in the soap opera and their relative equality seems to have inhibited the

Situation comedy: Shirley (Cindy Williams) and Laverne (Penny Marshall) on "Laverne and Shirley." Photo: Copyright © 1981, Paramount Pictures.

rise of major archetypes among them. The absence of star names, an effect of budget restrictions, is another explanation for this phenomenon. Perhaps most important, the everyday content of the soap operas necessitated by daily programming may also prevent the emergence of the more extravagantly fantastic and neurotic mythical patterns that inform the universe of the evening adventure series or domestic comedy. It seems that the more undistinguished characters of soap opera are regarded as ordinary people one knows exceedingly well rather than as superhuman inhabitants of a fantasy world.

A special category of this dramatic universe of myth is that of the Saturday morning cartoon films for children. These cartoons are openly mythical both in their animal characters and in their primitive demons and omnipotent children who populate the violent, often debased science and space fiction so prevalent in this world. This is the segment of American television that seems to me to be the most obviously harmful, both socially and culturally. Here the minds and imaginations of children are being systematically debased. The traditional fairy stories that these cartoons seem to have replaced were also often violent and portrayed self-centered characters (the youngest child who finally gets his way), but these elements in the traditional fairy tale or the better children's fiction of later times were generally accompanied by fine language, poetic imagery, and an underlying tenderness absent from today's cartoon fare. It is precisely because the basic features of these cartoons appeal to negative tendencies present in all children that they are so harmful, for they miss the opportunity which a more imaginative and poetic treatment of the same themes would provide to educate children's tastes and imaginations.

### Commercial Patterns

Beyond all these mythic series—the adventure series, the domestic situation comedy, the soap opera, and the children's cartoon shows—there lies a further area of explicitly dramatized material that is even more significant than all the preceding in the molding of our consciousness and the shaping of our daily lives: that is the world of the television commercial.

Not only are the great majority of commercials directly dramatic in nature (playlets of mere seconds' duration), but most of those that at first sight appear nondramatic contain the basic elements of fictional drama. Let us start with the most obviously dramatic kind of commercial, which usually follows a rigidly prescribed three-beat pattern. The sufferer from hemorrhoids, or bad breath, or an inability to make good coffee is near despair and appeals to a friend or relative for help; the friend draws the sufferer's attention to a product. There follows a moment of insight: this headache powder contains more of a painkilling ingredient than any other! this chewing gum fights bad breath more energetically! This moment of insight (the *anagnorisis* of classical drama) results in a reversal of fortune (the *peripateia*) so that in the third beat we now find the erstwhile sufferer relieved, restored, and as a result blissfully happy, free from pain, anxiety, and guilt and able to make good coffee and thus capable of keeping her husband at home rather than have him roam the taverns in search of solace in drink or at the bosom of another woman, etc. This happy resolution is usually followed by the appearance of the product's symbol or trademark accompanied by a song or jingle, corresponding to the appearance in classical drama of the *deus ex machina* and the final choral ode that provide the resolution to apparently insoluble difficulties.

There are other types of dramatic structure among the commercials. One variation is what we might call the *analytical* structure, which reveals the tragic events of the past only through their reflection in a present situation. The archetypal pattern is the beautiful girl who tells us she was ugly until she discovered a certain shampoo, lipstick, eyeshadow, etc. Here again an obviously fictional character presents us with a brief glimpse into a situation that was fraught with peril—indeed, tragedy—until a moment of insight brought the solution that resulted in the heroine's present happiness. Here too the choral song or jingle and the symbolic *deus ex machina* frequently appear.

Closely allied to this type is the one in which a "real" person—a film star or athlete—tells his or her story or directly recommends a product or service. Are these not "real" people? Yes and no, but mainly no. They clearly are not recounting real experiences; we know that they are unlikely to owe their present beauty or success to the product or service they are endorsing, and we know that they are speaking a text written by highly skilled writers. Clearly they are acting, though they might be acting out their public personae (which may be quite different from their real personalities). If, for example, the late John Wayne appeared as the rugged frontiersman recommending the thrift induced by putting one's money into a certain savings institution, it was abundantly clear that he was appearing as the embodiment of all the cowboys and sheriffs he had enacted in fictional stories rather than as the private John Wayne. The same is true of the other folk heroes who make commercial endorsements. In fact, of course, the impact of a commercial of this type does not derive from its explicit content, but rather from the famous person's association with the product. The public realizes that the institution concerned has enough money to pay the star's immense fees—and can infer that it must be very powerful indeed to command such a star to speak for it. Here too we are in a mythical universe: a demigod who can be made to serve an institution reflects upon its glory, lends it his aura.

Other forms of commercial mini-dramas include the musical number, in which the benefits of the product or service are enacted in song and dance, often around an allegorical representation of the power embodied within it; the allegorical drama enacted by actors or cartoon figures (incarnations of dirt, engine corrosion, pain, or bad odors), puppets, or animals with human attributes (singing cats, dogs, or chimpanzees); the mythicization of objects—the car or pizza displayed in preternatural beauty or succulence, accompanied by song or dithyrambic jingle.

These types of commercial—and some intermediate and

related variations—constitute the vast bulk of TV advertising. If the heroes and heroines, the villains and bunglers of dramatic series belong to a universe of mythical legend, the world of the commercials is an even more profoundly *real* region of the mythical universe of our civilization. For here we are in the presence of demigods and divine powers. And, on reflection, it becomes clear that this truly is a religious kind of drama. The religion involved is none other than that of *animism*—the belief that objects of everyday use are inhabited by powers that may be benevolent or hostile and must be appeased to induce them to take our side. We can observe in commercials the same dissociation of consciousness that we have already noticed in the process by which the characters of soap operas and dramatic series are perceived as being both fictional and, at the same time, more real than real. The individuals who watch commercials—and act on their urging, consciously or subconsciously—know that the ingredients in a detergent are merely chemicals, virtually the same as those contained in most other detergents. Yet they respond to the spoken or sung assertion that a given detergent contains a miraculous ingredient, that there is a special goodness in a shampoo, that a well-known actor, merely because he used to play a doctor in a series, can give expert advice in matters of health and personal hygiene.

The commercials are more than a mere marginal ingredient in American television. They are in fact the lifeblood and the *raison d'être* of all the other commercial programming. They are also the most costly and most elaborately produced ingredient on TV and its most ubiquitous element. All other programs exist to attract viewers to the commercials.

That the world—the metaphysics—portrayed or implied in the commercials is real, in the sense that it actually shapes the actions and decisions of millions of people, is attested to by the very fact that they are there and that the whole vast financial edifice of a gigantic industry is built on them. No one would invest the enormous sums that are spent on the production of commercials if they did not work, if they did not achieve their intended results. And the overwhelming use of the dramatic mode of communication rather than the

Superman saves the day on "The Superfriends Hour." Superman is a registered trademark of DC Comics Inc. and is used with permission. Photo: Copyright © 1981, DC Comics Inc.

discursive in TV commercials is in itself further evidence of the immense increase in the use and importance of drama in our time, of the veritable explosion of dramatic expression that characterizes our epoch.

Commercials, more than any other ingredient of the television programming schedule, exemplify the special characteristics and advantages of drama as a method of communication: above all, its ability to compress into a single instant a very large number of items of information—most of which are perceived subliminally, as a general gestalt with a strong emotional impact. In a commercial drama lasting only thirty seconds, every detail is of critical importance: the housewife serving a breakfast cereal to her brood of children must be attractive enough to elicit emulation but not so attractive as to preclude identification on the part of innumerable average-looking women; the furnishings of the kitchen in which the scene takes place, the garden glimpsed through the window, the children's faces and clothes, the background music all must make their powerful statement within the span of a few seconds. What is being projected here is something like an *ideal* world, in the sense that, as in Plato's philosophy, the ideal is more real than the "real," which is manifested in this degraded world only in imperfect representations of the ideal, eternal, archetypal reality.

The playwright Bertolt Brecht advocated the use of drama as an instrument of social engineering, a powerful teaching tool to change people's lives. Brecht was an adherent of the behaviorist school and based much of his theory of the didactic drama on assumptions derived from that branch of psychology. It is ironic that the truest fulfillment of Brecht's postulates of a didactic drama designed to convert mankind to Communism—which Brecht himself outlined in a highly speculative and unscientific way—should have come in the TV commercials of capitalism (whatever that term may still mean), for these commercials are, in a highly scientific and experimental manner, derived from empirical research carried out on the basis of behaviorist methodology. Commercials are the true didactic drama of our age, a drama that powerfully affects the way of life of the millions of spectators indoctrinated through it.

Television is perceived by its viewers as a form of relaxation, of entertainment. But insofar as TV forms an important part of their consciousness, insofar as it can be regarded as their collective daydream, and insofar as the denizens of that daydream, through their omnipresence and their continuous existence over long periods of time, become the equivalent of mythic archetypes, ultimately all that world of fiction, that realm of entertainment, assumes a highly concrete reality. It is real because it shapes people's actions: the heroes of its sagas become models of human conduct; the underlying assumptions of their behavior become implied or explicit ethical maxims governing people's decisions on how to live their lives. The overheated, hysterical urgings of commercials form the basis of their ideas on how to shape their environment.

Moreover, the identity of a culture, the self-image of a nation, is formed by the concepts, myths, beliefs, and patterns of conduct that are instantly recognized by the members of that social entity as being peculiarly theirs. No other single factor of our present-day civilization—not the educational system or religion or science or the arts—is so all-pervasive, so influential, so totally accessible to and shared by all individuals in society as is the world presented by television. Indeed, a true diagnosis of the ills of society might well start from a serious consideration of the world as presented on television. Different individuals have been exposed to different types of schools, different religious teachings, different socioeconomic milieus, different levels of conversation and discourse. But they all, almost without exception, have been exposed to and nurtured by the world as mirrored in television. Television is the *one* factor that practically all the individuals in this society have in common. It is the unifying substratum of experience. In this sense television—and above all the fictional world that informs it—is a dominant ingredient shaping our consciousness of reality.

Chicago police and dissenting youths during riots that disrupted the 1968 Democratic National Convention.

# 4

# Reality into Fiction

A FRENCH AVANT-GARDE PLAY of the late sixties depicted a family, fascinated and thrilled by a war going on in the street below their flat, feeling immensely privileged that their windows gave them a far better view of the skirmishes, ambushes, and executions than did those of their neighbors, who had to crane their necks to get a glimpse of the action. When, however, the war finally invaded their own apartment and confronted them with death and disaster on their hitherto inviolate territory, the members of this family were not only shocked and aggrieved but also indignant that events that had been no more than a thrilling entertainment for them should actually turn out to *involve* them as well. The play, *Tomorrow, from Any Window* by Jean-Claude Grumberg, demonstrated an important aspect of the television age and its consciousness, for the television set is just such a window upon "life": wars, revolutions, floods, earthquakes, an endless series of upheavals and calamities.

Long before the advent of television violent and traumatic events provided material for thrilling stories eagerly absorbed as a welcome diversion by people unaffected by the events themselves. In Goethe's *Faust* two fat and complacent burghers taking an Easter promenade discourse on the pleasure of being able to hear that "far down in Turkey whole nations crash into each other" while they themselves remain snug and comfortable, knowing that they are immune from such shocks. Reality in all its harshness and horror has always been turned into narratives in which fact becomes a kind of fiction, tales of faraway events and places, in short, "history."

## The Age of the Eyewitness

Nevertheless television has brought about a radical change in the manner and mode of this process: written accounts, illustrated with drawings or still photographs, put events into perspective and give the recipient of the information a chance to see them as a whole and in the light of reflection; the TV picture, by contrast, takes the viewer directly to the scene of the action and shows it to him as it occurs, in all its closeness and immediacy, so that he feels actually present on the battlefield, at the scene of the demonstration, at the launching of the space rocket. The written account usually combines description with reflection and quiet assessment and is meant to be read in detached solitude; the television image is *drama*, an event experienced by an eyewitness who is emotionally involved and much too close to be able to see the event whole or in a larger context that would enable him to evaluate its true significance.

Moreover television, like all drama, concentrates and intensifies its action by highlighting scenes with the greatest visual and emotional impact, including scenes of violence, while neglecting material that develops slowly or lacks visual drama. In a political demonstration that might have lasted several hours, for example, the thirty seconds during which the policemen's batons were raining down on a group of protesters might be the only episode televised of the entire incident. What is more, that brief segment will be edited in a manner that will give the episode a structure of mounting tension to make it even more dramatic.

There can be no doubt that in a society where most people take most of their information about current events from the TV screen, the public perception of what is going on in the world will be substantially different from that in a society where most information is absorbed through the written word and static illustrations. There is, above all, a shift of emphasis from the large perspective to the isolated incident; a loss of abstract insight as against a greater immediacy in the perception of details selected as often as not by criteria independent of their significance within the whole picture.

Statistics, for example, are notoriously undramatic. Large numbers, whether spoken by an announcer or illustrated in the form of diagrams or moving graphics, remain abstract and lacking in emotional impact. A television picture of a single starving child, on the other hand, will inevitably have a great emotional effect, regardless of whether that child is one of a hundred famine victims, or one of a thousand or tens of thousands. The availability or accessability of such pictures may seriously distort the TV public's—and the world's—awareness of the overall situation. An area that happens to make the news—because a camera team chanced to be in the vicinity or because the location lay en route to another assignment—may leap into the center of world attention, while other famine areas with greater needs and suffering are ignored. In recent years, for example, considerable attention was focused on the famine in Kampuchea (because it was big news in the aftermath of the Vietnam War and within easy access of Thailand) while severe famines in the drought areas of Central Africa received little or no TV coverage for a long while.

The lack of flexibility, moreover, in the duration of news programs, imposed by the rigidities of TV scheduling, necessitates a high degree of selectivity in the editorial decisions of the news producers. This, in turn, results in highly arbitrary choices even among those items that promise the most visual excitement and drama, while those stories that may be more important in terms of their long-term significance but have little visual, dramatic impact may receive cursory attention. And perhaps—from the television professional's point of view—rightly so. Not only is it very difficult to make abstract issues vivid and exciting on television, but it simply may not be possible for the medium to communicate them

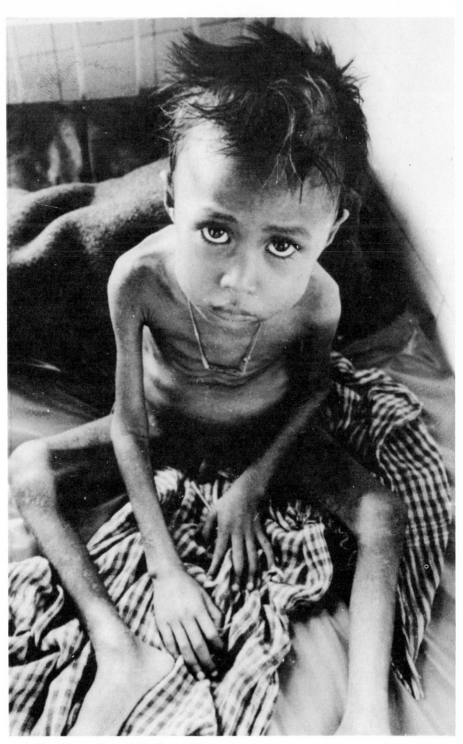

A starving Kampuchean child. Photo: UPI.

very well at all. For example, during the period preceding the 1975 referendum on Britain's decision to join the European Economic Community (EEC), British television made a determined effort to explain to its viewers the complex regulations and operating methods of the EEC and their likely impact upon life in Britain and the country's future economic development. Because the forces for and against the Common Market were allotted equal time to put forth their cases, there was a surfeit of material in all possible forms—discussions, lectures with diagrams, documentary films on industrial and agricultural questions, etc. At the end of this voluminous and protracted campaign there was a general consensus among expert observers that the whole undertaking had produced only a minimal increase in the public's understanding of the issues involved and that the result of the referendum (which was won overwhelmingly by the promarket faction) was largely attributable to the voters' inclination to follow the government line. All the hours of patient indoctrination, explanation, and elucidation seemed to have hardly dented the general ignorance. Whether the programs concerned had simply failed to dramatize the issues sufficiently or whether people had switched off broadcasts that promised to be dry and abstract is difficult to tell. What the episode highlights is the difficulty the medium encounters when it attempts to transmit complex, abstract information. While it is no doubt possible that better ways of structuring such TV programs can and will be found, the basic problem derives from the attitude of viewers to the medium they regard basically as a purveyor of entertainment.

### The Entertainment Principle vs. the Reality Principle

And here we have come to the heart of the matter: in essence a dramatic medium, television from the beginning has been compelled by the special requirements of its nature—its own inner logic—to put its emphasis on material with a dramatic, emotional, personalized content. TV therefore is perceived by its audience primarily as a medium of *entertainment*, and all programming—including the news, documentaries, and political broadcasts—is ultimately judged for its *entertainment value.* The effect is that material about events in the real world has to compete, as entertainment, with the openly fictional material radiated incessantly which constitutes the collective daydreams of the masses. Embedded in a never-ending stream of such material, these fragments of reality, glimpsed through the framed stage of the TV set, merge into the world of fantasy with which TV is preoccupied. The distinctions between daydream and reality are again blurred and distorted.

What are the main psychological benefits the viewer of dramatic entertainment craves? First is excitement in the form of suspense that makes him forget the passing of time; the thrills that come from empathy with characters facing danger and imminent disaster; the relief when the good defeat the forces of evil. Equally important and powerful are the cathartic effects of the "beautiful" emotions, such as patriotic pride, religious uplift, tearful joy at the union of a happy, loving couple, and even the gentle sadness of partings and bereavements. And third there is the craving for amusement, laughter, lights, glamour. These, inevitably, are the criteria by which the offerings of an entertainment medium will be judged. And if those elements in the programming that are meant to achieve quite a different end, namely to convey information about the real world, are perceived as just another ingredient in that vast entertainment package they also will, inevitably, tend to be judged by the same criteria: a good news broadcast will be the one that contains the maximum of excitement, high emotion, and amusement.

In the sphere of excitement, however, there operates a law of diminishing returns: the more accustomed viewers become to violence, the more violent the violence has to become to make an impact. This holds true for the news as well as for prime-time dramatic series. Violence produces "good" television. And because the editors of news programs are constantly in pursuit of stories that have a strong visual and dramatic element, violence is assured of a central place in any news show. To me it seems overwhelmingly clear that the increase in terrorism, bombings, assassinations, kidnap-

*"Don't you understand? This is <u>life</u>, this is what is happening.
We <u>can't</u> switch to another channel."*

Drawing by Robt. Day; © 1970
The New Yorker Magazine, Inc.

pings, and the taking of hostages is closely and organically connected with the nature of television and its rise to its present position as the principal information medium in the world. We have grown accustomed to modern-day outlaws demanding TV time.

But that is by no means the most important aspect of the matter. The *drama*, the intensity of the suspense, and the ongoing news potential of the unfolding events that actions such as embassy takeovers and hostage-taking provide give the perpetrators of these actions an almost ideal field for publicizing themselves, especially when the moment for the final assault or hostage exchange arrives and everything is in place and can be fully and minutely shown on the TV screen. Calculate, for instance, the prime air time an action like the taking of the American hostages in Tehran gave the Iranian terrorists and translate it into the sums that commercials of similar duration would have cost: such a terrorist act is worth literally tens of millions of dollars of free publicity. It is no wonder that the incidence of such terrorism has multiplied throughout the world.

*In the end the terrorists might be said to be actually working for television* by providing the thrills and the violence that enable the news shows to compete with fictional thrillers and an endless stream of often sadomasochistic drama. The men and women who run television news programs are honorable citizens and compassionate human beings (I count some of them among my friends), but when a disaster occurs somewhere in the world a gleam of excitement and exhilaration comes into their eyes as the report flashes over the telex. The

American hostages shown being paraded by their militant Iranian captors in Tehran, November 4, 1979. Photo: UPI.

nature of the medium makes this inevitable. A day without a disastrous event is a dull day and will produce a dull broadcast, and a dull broadcast will to them equal personal, professional failure.

There can be no doubt that those who are unscrupulous enough to resort to violence as a means of getting publicity exploit this state of affairs. The tactics of street demonstrators and protesters are dominated by such considerations: route a Nazi or Ku Klux Klan procession through a predominantly Jewish or black neighborhood and you are certain to arouse well-founded expectations of violence that bring out television cameras in force. A phone call to a television news editor promising fisticuffs and fireworks may well secure air time worth many thousands of dollars in free publicity.

Here, then, the nature of television as an entertainment medium, a purveyor of daydreams that transmutes reality into a kind of fictional drama, actually dictates the development of events in the real world. To a certain extent analogous considerations have always played a part: kings and knights of old may have set out on spectacular exploits in the hope of becoming immortalized in an epic poem or a ballad. But in our world today the deliberate creation of sensational events has become a *major* factor in the shaping of developments in the real world, a factor not to be ignored, although very difficult to deal with.

It has been argued that television and other news media should simply ignore the actions of terrorists and not report them at all. This is the practice in the totalitarian countries of the Soviet bloc, where anything that might publicize such tactics is severely restricted if not entirely suppressed and where even plane crashes are not reported, though for different reasons (such information would diminish the official picture of state efficiency and technological superiority). But in the West, coverage of events that have actually taken place cannot be suppressed. Somebody will inevitably report them. In a field like TV where there is competition for the best, the most exciting, and the most entertaining, it would clearly be unthinkable to ignore such dramatic events or to relegate them to a low place on the totem pole.

## Politics Behind a Glass Screen

The viewer who from his grandstand seat at the TV window sees wars, acts of terrorism, murders, and executions—reality turned into thrilling entertainment—is kept in a schizophrenic state of mind the reverse of that produced by soap operas and series, which are fictions perceived not only as fictions but also, at the same time, as realities that are more real than events in the real world. For although the viewer is aware of the reality of the news and documentary material, he nevertheless is also instinctively judging it as though it were fiction. The process may not be a conscious one, but it goes on nevertheless and is observable in the degree of attention (or inattention) given a news broadcast and in the tendency to switch channels if the events being reported are perceived as uninteresting.

It might be asked, for example, to what extent the decreasing interest in U.S. domestic politics is attributable to the influence of television. Can it be that the political material on television suffers by comparison with the more interesting and involving fictional fare that occupies so much air time? Or might it be that the politicians, however much they may now be selected (as they undoubtedly are) on grounds of their attractiveness and drawing power on television, rarely match the glamour and erotic appeal of actors whose whole training and outlook is directed toward producing the maximum of personal magnetism, and who, moreover, are seen in interesting and exciting situations? Or, indeed, might the whole political process—perceived as a show to be passively ingested from the television screen—seem utterly remote and, behind that impenetrable window, beyond the influence of individual participation or involvement? These questions may never be finally and unequivocably answered but they must be asked; they must be considered and weighed.

If politicians, by and large, seem remote and uninteresting on the screen, it is all the more remarkable and significant that the network anchormen and anchorwomen of television *do* succeed in holding the attention of viewers and commanding their loyalties and confidence. This is, as I have

The anchorman as father-figure: Walter Cronkite on "CBS Evening News." Photo: Courtesy of CBS.

noted previously, a function of their ability to act, to project a personality that may well be an invention different from the broadcaster's private self. But here also it is their familiarity, the frequency and regularity with which they appear, that creates their impact. While the pictures of the real world they present take on the qualities of fiction, their own television personalities become more and more real. They are talked about, adored, quoted, and trusted. The immense salaries these individuals command in a hardheaded commercial world attest to the real power of the illusion they have succeeded in creating.

## News as Entertainment

If the national news in the United States is concerned mainly with national and world stories and the drama and violence of international relations, the local news—such a staple of the television scene in the U.S., where television service is far more decentralized than in most other Western nations—deals mainly with crime and violence on the local level, in much the same fashion, with the more dramatic and sensational stories occupying the foreground. The local news programs, because they are concerned with a smaller geographic area and relatively more mundane material, have become increasingly preoccupied with entertaining their audiences with amusing and titillating features. On an uneventful day with little important news, items have to be invented or created. The local anchormen and anchorwomen take the opportunity to groom their well-loved personalities and cultivate their audience allegiance. They will, especially on slow news days, give practical advice, interact with local characters, highlight amusing features of their area. Even the meteorologist is often turned into a personality: a comedian or clown, or, if female, a sex bomb. These attempts are not always successful, which suggests that the number of people with the actor's ability to project an interesting and intriguing personality is limited or that management has misperceived what the viewing audience finds appealing.

## The Documentary Dilemma

News programs by their very nature tend to be "bitty." As they have to cover the widest possible range of the day's events, they can never treat a subject in much depth. There is thus an immense potential in the medium for longer, in-depth documentaries that might provide the public with the background to the complex issues that lie behind the individual news event, say, the Russian invasion of Afghanistan. How many viewers, for example, have any idea of the long and complex background of the struggle throughout the nineteenth century between the Russians and the British to establish control over that vital area between the Russian Empire and India, the British expeditions into the country that were defeated by the Afghans, the endless fighting in the area around the Khyber Pass? Similarly, there are numerous domestic issues that deserve treatment at length and in depth. In a commercial system like that in the U.S. such programs have become relatively rare: they are extremely costly to produce and do not promise high ratings. Most of the documentaries of this kind are seen on the Public Broadcasting Service and tend to be imported from Britain, Canada, and other countries with publicly financed TV services.

Many of these—and some of the rare "specials" that are produced in the U.S.—succeed in providing insights and deepening understanding. But even in this area of programming the temptation to overdramatize and trivialize is clearly present. Take the example of a recent British documentary about the criteria used to establish when a person can be declared legally dead and how this may affect potential donors of transplant organs. The program's contention that there is a danger that accident victims who are still alive might be wrongly pronounced dead—developed in a sensational manner—led to a dangerous drop in the number of potential donors. The British Medical Association claimed that the subject had been seriously misrepresented in a desire to produce an exciting program. When the BBC offered the BMA the right to reply, the medical organization refused on the grounds that the time made available was too short to deal with so extraordinarily complex a matter.

Whatever the rights and wrongs in this specific case, it illustrates the dangers of this kind of investigative TV journalism. Television documentaries, even those of the extended, in-depth variety, face rigid time pressures owing to the nature of the programming process. An investigative book can reach its organic length, as can a documentary film for cinema showing, whereas their television counterpart, with only rare exceptions, cannot: it must be planned to conform to its preordained, fixed time slot. Moreover, there is also the limitation of the medium itself, its resistance to abstraction and its pull toward personalization. Even so serious and public-spirited a series as the BBC's "Civilisation" could be criticized on the grounds that there was a danger that the subject matter would be eclipsed by the star quality of the personality of its presenter, Sir Kenneth Clark.

The recent TV magazine programs that local and network news departments have developed exhibit the same characteristics to an even greater degree. Designed to be dipped into rather than watched with concentration, they often trivialize their material—insofar as it was not trivial from the outset—and present little more than a glimpse of the personalities shown or a faint taste of the issues or activities with which they are involved.

## A Personality Showcase

The same happens with discussion and interview programs, although here more time can be devoted to issues. In the more ambitious discussion programs where a politician or public figure is questioned by journalists, the guest can give some account of his or her ideas and policies. Yet what the audience takes away even from this kind of show is more likely to be an impression of the guest's personality, his fluency, his ability to evade embarrassing issues, his deftness of reaction—in other words, a portrait of his character—rather than a coherent understanding of the issues discussed. The lighter, more trivial interview programs, the talk shows, devoted largely to entertainment, publicizing forthcoming stage or TV appearances or movies or books of well-known show-business personalities, exhibit these characteristics in a more blatant form.

These talk shows and the game shows they sometimes resemble can be assigned to the category of improvised popular drama in which, throughout history, stereotyped characters have played for laughs within a more or less predictable structural framework, be it that of the commedia dell'arte, *Hanns Wurst* play, vaudeville, or circus clowns' interludes between acts. In the game shows this is combined with the built-in drama of a competition for sumptuous prizes and the raw emotions among the contestants provoked by winning and losing.

Though game shows are usually laughed off by their sponsors as being "good clean fun," they seem to me a deplorable manifestation of our culture. Not only are many of them clearly sadomasochistic in that they encourage enjoyment derived from the humiliation and embarrassment of the participants (and in some cases from the embarrassing exposure of intimate details of their participants' lives, as in those involving newlywed couples), but the underlying assumptions of many of the game concepts have disquieting implications. They stress the value of relatively unimportant tidbits of information. And the condescending manner of some of the "hosts" underscores the disquieting features of these programs and makes me think of them as a modern equivalent of the gladiatorial contests of ancient Rome.

### The Drama of Sport

The area where the real and the dramatic merge most successfully is in the realm of sports. All spectator sports involving competition contain a built-in element of drama—all sports competitions are after all stylized wars, fictionalized struggles—and are structured in a manner calculated to produce the maximum amount of suspense and excitement. As they are invariably concerned with physical activity, sports also emphasize TV's basically erotic orientation, whether in the direction of sadomasochistic eroticism, as in the more violent forms of sports like boxing and wrestling, or simply by displaying beautiful bodies in graceful action. Witness the increase in the popularity of gymnastics after it had been introduced to television audiences within the framework of the 1972 Olympic games: the spectacular gymnasts like Olga Korbut became instant heroes and heroines among people who previously would have regarded gymnastics as an unexciting sport, if they had thought about it at all. Television similarly brought figure skating, ice dancing, and a number of other sports into sudden prominence.

Although the people, the contest, and the prizes in sports are real, the structure of the competition is severely formalized and basically dramatic—both on the playing field and, even more so, on the TV screen. Television, through close-ups and instant replays, and through mini-interviews with the protagonists, brings the participants in the sports drama closer to the spectator than does attendance at the actual event. In the stadium there is drama seen at a distance, but on television the participants can become characters closely akin to those in a play, and, as fantasy figures in the collective daydream, perform superhuman feats of strength and endurance.

## Commercials: Fantasy and the Hard Sell

Where fantasy and reality are fused more deeply and inextricably than in any other area of programming, however, is in the commercials. Commercials are drama that turns into reality; they are also reality presented as fantasy. The playlets of the commercials are designed to exert the power of fantasy to make people spend real money on real products. They simultaneously convert those products into agents dispensing imaginary satisfactions; they mythologize real products into quasi-magical agents. The soft drink, the wine, the glass of sparkling water become elixirs of implied delights with associated psychological benefits yielding pleasures beyond their positive material effects (if such can be postulated to exist in the first place).

## False Consciousness

Fantasies, of course, while being unreal, nonetheless have a powerful and concrete influence on reality: for it is fantasy that often determines human beings' actions in the concrete world of reality. Television's ability—or tragic tendency—to turn reality into a kind of fantasy thus in turn, as previously noted, has its influence and impact on events and developments in the real world. The danger lies in the "false consciousness"—the *fausse conscience* in Sartre's sense—that television produces, which results in attitudes toward the real world that are unrealistic, illusionary, and even harmful. The way TV's treatment of the news publicizes and thus seems actually to inspire the increase in political terrorism is but one case in point. There are many others. For example, to what extent did the TV coverage of the Vietnam War, and of

Demonstrators en route to an anti-Vietnam War rally at San Francisco's Kezar Stadium, April 1972. Photo: UPI.

the protest movement against it, in highlighting the horrors of the war on the one hand, overstressing the revulsion of public opinion at home on the other, actually lead to what may, in the long run, turn out to have been a wrong course of action—namely the premature abandonment of the struggle? The Vietnam War was the first war in history to be fully reported on television. Was the image of that war as conveyed to the American public a true one, true not only in showing the horrors of warfare but also in putting them into the correct context? And did not the protesters make, also probably for the first time in history, full and highly intelligent use of the medium's predilection for violent, dramatic images, in creating, quite deliberately, what they called *street theater:* dramatic events that would have the optimal effect on television and compel the maximum exposure for their cause?

Every society has—and is shaped by—its self-image. It seems to me beyond doubt that television plays a significant role in shaping that collective self-image. And I would argue that the image of the U.S. that is presented on television is a false one: more violent, shallow, vulgar than reality; and, above all, pervaded by the hysterical tone of a perpetual hard sell quite unlike the far more relaxed atmosphere of real American life.

The presentation of such a distorted self-image to the rising generation must give cause for anxiety. And so must the fact that, owing to the great popularity of American television programs abroad and their relative cheapness and vast quantity, this image of the society is being exported worldwide to populations who have little chance of correcting and modifying it by direct observation. Both inside and outside the United States, the image of the society displayed by television is bound to have far-reaching cultural and political consequences.

# 5

# The Long-term Effects of Television

TELEVISION IS A TECHNOLOGICAL MIRACLE, a wonderful new instrument of communication, capable of widening and enlarging mankind's horizons. It has given each individual a powerful means of increasing his or her awareness of the world and of his or her fellow human beings. It has made entertainment a basic human right, available, on tap and on demand, at virtually any hour of the day or night. It has changed the life-style and daily habits of all who have received it into their homes.

There can be no doubt that as an instrument of communication and information television is of the utmost potential value. The sheer volume of information supplied with even the shallowest program is immense. Children who grow up with television obtain information from everything they watch on TV—cartoons, commercials, even the trashiest of films. Through television, the old, infirm, and lonely can be made to feel that they are in contact with other human beings, that they remain in touch with events around them.

The medium, moreover, has a vast potential to enrich people's lives by giving them access to sports and the arts: it can make activities they may at first watch passively so attractive that they are stimulated into active participation. There is even considerable evidence that television can stimulate reading. The sales of books adapted for and dramatized on television often increase markedly during the run of such mini-series.

Although many of these positive qualities and achievements of television are already in evidence and others hold promise of future benefit, the long-term impact of the less beneficial aspects of television cannot be ignored. Many of these more negative effects of TV derive from its basic nature as a dramatic medium.

Most of TV viewing, as I have tried to show, is akin to daydreaming. Why should the "collective daydreaming" of TV be different from, or worse than, the individual daydreaming people have succumbed to from time immemorial? There certainly is much force in the argument that such mass-produced collective daydreams are bound to be less healthy and beneficial than the individual daydreams that respond to the specific needs of the persons concerned, serve as a compensating self-therapy for their psychological difficulties, and feed their individual imaginations. Mechanically mass-produced fantasies will inevitably tend to be reductionistic, homogenizing individual needs and inhibiting the growth of integrated personalities.

The psychological effects of a phenomenon like television are notoriously difficult to establish on an experimental basis. Even if it were possible to measure, for example, the lessening of a sense of reality or a sense of self in present-day populations as compared with those of a century ago (which clearly it is not), the sheer number of factors contributing to such a change would be far too large to allow the isolation of a single element as the one mainly responsible. There have been too many other changes in the cultural climate in addition to the advent of television: a spectacular rise in the standard of living; great improvements in education, social services, housing, and means of transportation; important developments in political organization; changes in attitudes on morality—not to mention the changes brought about by wars and historical upheavals. Nevertheless some conclusions, however speculative, do emerge from close observation of these changes.

## Quality vs. Quantity

Among teachers and educators in the U.S., for example, there is general agreement that the attention span of students has diminished noticeably over the past two decades. And there is evidence that this disturbing trend is related to the frequent commercial interruptions on television programs that the children view. Similarly, there is considerable agreement that a decline in the ability of students to concentrate while reading has simultaneously occurred, even among those who are highly intelligent and motivated. A 1980 study involving half a million sixth- to twelfth-grade students, conducted by the California Department of Education, demon-

Kunta Kinte (LeVar Burton) in the TV mini-series adaptation of Alex Haley's *Roots*. Photo: Courtesy of The Wolper Organization, Inc.

strated a strong statistical link between high levels of TV watching (three hours or more per day) and low achievement test scores. The more TV the children watched, the lower their average scores, regardless of the number of hours they spent reading and doing homework. If these are, indeed, the early consequences of television watching on a generation of children who have grown up with TV practically from birth, the cumulative effects over several generations, when these children's children grow up in home environments created by parents already so debilitated, are bound to be increasingly serious.

Equally important is the problem of the impact of images of sex and violence on the viewing audience. The frequent attempts by psychologists, sociologists, government committees, and others to devise experimental procedures by which this impact might be measured and quantified have, on the whole, produced no decisive conclusions. Although the 1970 report of the Presidential Commission on Obscenity and Pornography exonerated pornography as a cause of antisocial behavior, two recent studies—at the University of Wisconsin and the University of Manitoba—indicate that viewers of filmed sexual violence are provoked to more aggressive behavior, especially toward women. In the University of Manitoba experiment, the findings indicated that this heightened aggressiveness persists for at least a week. Yet even if it is established with certainty that a week after watching a pornographic film depicting sexual violence a group of human subjects reacts violently when exposed to a real-life situation that is analogous to the events on the screen, we still do not know anything about the far more important question of what the likely effect of the film will be a year, five years, ten years hence; or conversely, whether the effect will have dissipated itself after another week or two. Nor do we know whether continuous exposure to such material has a cumulative effect, exerting an increasingly strong influence on the individual viewer's psyche and behavior, or whether, on the contrary, continuous exposure diminishes the long-term effect. Indeed, there are those who maintain that images of violence and sex on the screen have a cathartic effect, purging the viewer of anger and hostility, while others are equally convinced that television teaches the latent deviant the basics of assault and rape and incites him to imitative action.

Attempts to obtain quantified answers to these very serious questions through controlled experiments seem to me misconceived and futile. For almost four decades I was involved in the daily give-and-take of the BBC, which on a vast scale conducts its own research into audience responses. Documentary evidence of the reaction of individual audience members (in letters, interviews, etc.) indicates that there certainly are some people who *are* stimulated to antisocial behavior, while there are others, equally certainly, who find overt sex or violence on the screen cathartic. The problem lies in drawing a quantified distinction between the permissible and the inadmissible. If *one* viewer among millions were induced to commit a sex crime by watching a certain program, and ten thousand others felt relieved from sexual pressures as a result, would that justify the transmission of that program? Even if the answer to that question could be established with absolute certainty, which it cannot be, the ethical problem it poses would be no nearer a solution. In fact, quite the contrary: an affirmative answer would amount to a conscious decision to provoke that one sex crime.

It is abundantly clear that some programs are harmful to some people although, of course, it can never be established whether other stimuli—including reading, still photographs, or conversation—would not have been equally harmful. In puritanical environments where reading matter was limited, even the Bible and Shakespeare were frequently the source of sexual stimulation.

Children are especially vulnerable to explicit material of a violent or sexual nature. But here again the problems are virtually insoluble. As there is no way to guarantee that a given program will be totally inaccessible to children, should *all* television programming completely avoid any violent or sexual material? This is clearly impossible. There seems, moreover, to be a dangerous confusion about the nature of such material. The self-appointed guardians of "purity" in the media (cinema as well as television) almost invariably concentrate their attacks on explicitly sexual material. Yet, in fact, violence is just as—or even more dangerously—pornographic than nudity or sexual activity on the screen. Hence the material offered to children on American television, particularly the immensely violent and ugly cartoons, is to me among the most pornographic of all American broadcasting. Here too the argument that such cartoons are cathartic in ridding children of their violent impulses is frequently advanced. Though this may be true in the majority of cases, we are again left with the question of how large the minority might be that is actually harmed by this material and influenced to engage subsequently in violent behavior. The alarming increase in juvenile violence in the last two decades clearly suggests a connection between TV violence and youth crime. A recent study showed that violent incidents occur on American TV on an average of five times per hour during prime time and *eighteen times per hour* during weekend daytime children's programming.

Yet a quantitative approach that merely counts open references to sex or violent acts on the screen is in itself misleading. What matters is not the quantity but the quality of the material. Throughout the history of literature the treatment of these matters on a high artistic level has clearly produced effects that were far from harmful, but, on the contrary, had a deeply humanizing impact. It is not the subject matter per se that is important, but the seriousness and artistry with which it is treated. The blinding of Gloucester in *King Lear* and the murder of the old woman in Dostoevsky's *Crime and Punishment* are as violent as anything that popular television offers every day. What distinguishes scenes of brutality in the work of great artists from the daily fare offered on the mass medium of television is that the former reveal the horror of that violence, the suffering of the victims, and the anguish of the perpetrators of these brutal acts: they show the violence with all its complex human implications from the author's perspective of deep compassion. They depict violence within the context of a profoundly moral world view.

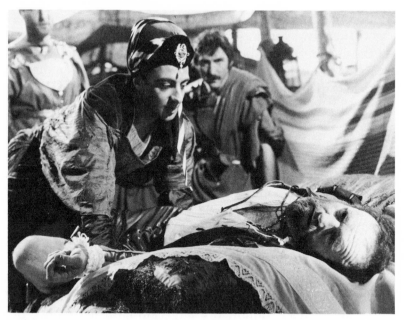

Violence within the context of a profoundly moral world view: Eros (Simon Chandler) and Anthony (Colin Blakely) in *Anthony and Cleopatra* on "The Shakespeare Plays."

Pornography can be defined as a distortion of reality through the isolation of certain acts by taking them out of a fully human context, by turning human beings into objects of mechanical operations. The description of an act of violence or a sexual act becomes pornography if the human context is eliminated, if no attention is given to the feelings of the adversary who is shot, of the woman who becomes the object of a sexual indulgence. The pornography of television is largely one of violence: the victims who fall under the hail of bullets in the final shoot-out scene of the typical crime episode have never been introduced as human beings; they never display any sign of suffering; they hardly ever even bleed. They fall like so many ninepins, to be counted with hoots of delight. We never learn whether they have relatives who would mourn them, aspirations that would show them to have been fully human.

The proliferation of cheap, dehumanized sex and violence on TV is bound, over the long run, to have a harmful effect, not merely in encouraging more violent actions on the part of TV viewers, but in gradually deadening the sensibilities of those exposed to such fare. Because television is basically a dramatic medium, no effort should be spared to make the immense quantity of dramatic material TV offers into better—*artistically* better—drama. Instead of blunting the sensibilities of viewers TV programs should treat human situations and characters with the complexity of real art in order to sharpen the perceptiveness of viewers and help them achieve greater sensitivity and understanding. This is not beyond the possible scope of a popular medium. Witness the great period of the early American cinema when Buster Keaton, Charlie Chaplin, Laurel and Hardy, D.W. Griffith, Douglas Fairbanks, and later, in the era of talkies, John Ford, Fritz Lang, and the Marx Brothers, to name only a few, produced works of real art that had the widest possible popular appeal while retaining a deep sense of humanity. The films of some of these artists also contained a large amount of violence but they were not, by any stretch of the imagination, dehumanizing or pornographic.

Television itself does occasionally rise to produce real works of art that, at the same time, can have the widest popular appeal: the fine television dramas of the fifties with original plays by notable dramatists are cases in point, as are the imported dramatizations of classical novels from the BBC or the work of brilliant comedians like Jack Benny or Bob Hope.

Of course, to demand that the vast quantity of material television requires to fill its steady stream of programming should all reach the level of genuine works of art is a counsel of perfection that must remain utopian. The economics and structure of the medium prohibit such an achievement. Nevertheless, as an aspiration, the demand for artistic quality, for more humanized and moral material to replace the endless stream of mechanically spewed out series and soap operas, must be in the forefront of the minds of all those who are concerned with the future of our culture. For lowered attention spans and loss of concentration pale in importance when compared to the numbing effects of long-term exposure to dehumanizing and simpleminded entertainment that debilitates the sensitivity of those who view it. It is often said that the material of American commercial TV is targeted at the mental level of a twelve-year-old child. Whether this is a consciously adopted policy or merely the outcome of a combination of market research and the producers' contempt for their audiences is relatively unimportant. What matters is that over a number of generations continuous exposure to such material is bound to result in a lowering of the general level of intelligence.

Yet our postindustrial age will require more and more highly trained and intelligent citizens. The quality of TV programming thus becomes a problem of major political and economic concern. It is a problem that is intimately linked with the future of education, for the educational process itself is affected by the material that children and young people are exposed to on TV, material that clearly has an immense influence on their perception of the world and their habits of thought.

Consider, for example, the quasi-magical world view underlying many television commercials: should a population whose future depends on its power of logical reasoning be continuously fed with the pseudoreasoning of commercials on the pattern of "This detergent will wash whiter because it contains a special ingredient that washes whiter"? And yet would such circular reasoning be tolerated if market research did not show it to be acceptable to—and effective upon—large masses of people? A population that feeds on, and accepts, this kind of spurious reasoning is in danger of sinking back into primitive modes of thought, the animistic state of preliterate societies.

One could actually argue with some force that, in fact, the bulk of the population of the world's developed countries has never emerged from such a preliterate stage, as serious newspapers and books have never been read by the majority of people; and that television, by being the first medium accessible to and eagerly assimilated by the masses, has merely made this fact more apparent. Yet even if this view is well founded, the pseudoreasoning of the commercials and their reliance on investing products with quasi-magical powers, the simplemindedness of most of the humor, the exploitation of the most basic thrills of violence and sexual titillation in the prime-time programming, in short, the primitiveness of the material offered by American television, must still give rise to anxiety—because for the first time the least intellectually developed segment of society is dictating the intellectual level of society's chief medium of information and communication. If comparatively few people read books or serious newspapers in previous times, at least the minority that *did* read them, which comprised the most influential citizens, conducted its intellectual life on a relatively high level. In our age, even the members of the intellectual elite are routinely exposed to TV and are expected to adapt to its level if they want to communicate through it.

### A Mirror of Society

It is also disquieting that in an age when we have the greatest access to our public leaders and their political programs, the percentage of eligible voters who take the trouble to go to the polls is declining steadily, and opinion surveys indicate that respect for politicians and political institutions is declining as well. This brings up important questions. Is this apathy bound up with the fact that on TV viewers see politicians in action more closely than in former times and that the politicians appear less heroic as a result? Or is it that television, which by its nature does not communicate abstract reasoning well, forces politicians to project their personalities rather than to discuss serious issues in depth, thus making the politicians appear shoddy and unconvincing? Or is it the distancing effect of the TV screen that reduces everything on it to a daydream, a world between fiction and reality, to be watched in passive apathy? More likely than not, all of these factors are involved in having produced what is an alarming trend.

The picture of politics as portrayed on the TV screen is only one facet of our society's image of itself that television conveys. The social ideology implicit in most of the programs broadcast on TV does not, I believe, express a true view of our culture, but what is in fact a distorted one. The effects of having this image constantly before us rather than a truer reflection of our basic social ethos and philosophy, as I have noted previously, must give cause for some apprehension. Certainly the younger generation nurtured on television is vulnerable to that image and the philosophy implicit within it: the image of a society concentrating on the hysterical hard sell and the frantic pursuit of material comfort, simplistic in its division of the world into good guys and bad guys, a society in which art and serious thought seem to have only a precarious foothold.

## Television Across Frontiers

The image of America as formulated on television is bound to have its effect not only on the society's self-image within the nation's borders, but also beyond them. Over the long run, the medium will undoubtedly have far-reaching effects on the shape of the cultural and even the political future of the world. Television already transcends many national borders and soon—with satellite transmission—will be able to do so even more.

Nations with powerful resources of talent and capital will be able to export their image, while small national and cultural units will increasingly be in danger of having their individuality swamped by those who can produce more—and more attractive—programming. This tendency is already making itself felt in many areas of the world. The United States, for example, has the largest output of television programs in the world and is, moreover, able to cover their cost on its very large home market. As a result the U.S. is able to export its programs at very low cost to other countries. Wherever one travels outside the Soviet bloc Kojak and Lucy, the Lone Ranger and Charlie's Angels, the Hulk and the astronauts of "Star Trek" can be seen on television screens in towns and villages. American popular culture has become a dominant influence in these areas: it shapes not only popular taste but life-styles. Blue jeans, Coca-Cola, rock music,

*Merger* by Robert Rauschenberg. 1962. Collection, The Museum of Modern Art, New York.

and hundreds of other American cultural phenomena are pressing back indigenous habits and products.

Television thus has what might be called a homogenizing effect on world culture: in many parts of the world indigenous folk songs fight a losing battle with rock and country music, indigenous cuisine with hamburgers and hot dogs. And this is true of the more highly developed countries of the West as well as of the nations of the Third World. Television endangers the cultural identity of many smaller or less populous Western nations, particularly those that border larger or more dominant political units with the same or a similar language. Canada has long battled the threat of being swamped by U.S. culture. Switzerland—whose German-speaking area borders two countries (Germany and Austria) with the same language, whose French-speaking area borders France, and whose Italian-speaking canton is next to Italy—is in an especially difficult situation. Belgium is in a similar position with regard to France and Holland. Populations of such nations who have the choice of looking at the news broadcasts of another country may well become more involved with that country's politics than with their own concerns, which may seem more small-time or more parochial. Even more threatening, from the point of view of the governments involved, is the fact that the population of East Germany greatly prefers West German television to what they are offered on their side of the Iron Curtain, that the areas of Czechoslovakia bordering Austria are so addicted to Austrian television that it is estimated that Austrian television may have more viewers in Czechoslovakia than does the Czech TV service. In turn, in many parts of Austria West German television is preferred to Austrian programs.

Even in countries like West Germany, France, and Britain a considerable proportion of TV programs come from the U.S. When the British Parliament passed the bill introducing commercial television to the United Kingdom (to compete with the BBC's public service), the bill contained a quota restricting the proportion of foreign (read American) material permitted to the new companies. American—and British—popular series are dubbed in German, French, and many other languages and constitute a large, and highly popular, ingredient in the programming of numerous countries.

It is thus no wonder that there is much talk abroad of American cultural imperialism, much anxiety among intellectuals concerned with the preservation of their indigenous cultures and national identities about the undoubted popularity and magnetism of the American folk culture among the masses of their countries. That the image of the United States exported in these programs is one of violence, gangsterism, and—in the situation comedies—a vulgar and materialistic outlook on life also has its influence on the way the United States is perceived abroad. Much of the anti-Americanism of many intellectuals in Europe, Asia, and Africa is derived from, or at least reinforced by, the ubiquity of American television material.

Conversely, in the United States, the importation of British programs to the financially starved Public Broadcasting Service has already given rise to comments, and complaints, about the intrusion of a foreign cultural influence. Witness too the concern of the American actors' union about the BBC/Time-Life Shakespeare series with its wholly British casting. The situation is aggravated by the fact that the kind of material imported from the BBC is precisely the more intellectual fare that is so meagerly represented on the American commercial networks, so that it sometimes seems as though the only cultural material available to American viewers originates in a foreign country. This brings up again the disquieting paucity on American commercial television of material that deals with what one might, in the widest sense, refer to as the area of high culture. The visual arts (painting and sculpture), architecture, serious literature, serious drama, and experimental theater are virtually excluded from the commercial networks and make only fitful appearances on public television.

## A Dictatorship of the Majority

Here lies one of American television's ultimate and particularly tragic paradoxes: television, being a visual and dramatic medium, is best suited to convey visual information and drama, but American commercial television makes practically no deliberate use of its potential in this direction. There is virtually no serious drama on American commercial television, while in other countries—West Germany, France, Britain, Scandinavia—television drama has become a major art form. (Important writers like Samuel Beckett, Eugene Ionesco, and Harold Pinter have written major works for television.) Nor is commercial television used in the U.S. to carry cultural information in the form of arts magazines, art films, or dramatized documentaries about great artists of the past, all of which form an important element in the television output of those European countries. Yet television has the potential to perform an important cultural service in these areas. In Britain, for example, it is a generally accepted fact that the upsurge of musical composition, performance, and concert-going is largely the outcome of the systematic presentation of serious music on the national radio networks over a period of a half century. Many of the playwrights of the British New Wave, which has produced an unprecedented flowering of serious drama since 1956, came from humble backgrounds and discovered their talents early, primarily through access to classical and modern drama on radio and television. In addition, the production of serious plays on radio and TV in Britain provides a training ground as well as a source of income for such young playwrights.

The justification often given for the absence of cultural material on American commercial TV is that it is of interest to only a minority of viewers and therefore has no place in a system that is compelled to maximize its audience to attract advertisers and achieve the largest possible revenues. But this kind of reasoning imposes a dictatorship of the majority while ignoring the tastes and needs of the minority. What would be the result if the same type of argument were applied in other closely related spheres? For example, why should great sums of money be spent on museums or libraries when only a tiny fraction of the population uses them? Even best-sellers reaching several million readers touch only a small percentage of the total population. If the scale of magnitude by which television audiences are measured were applied to these best-sellers, even they would not rate publication, let alone serious novels and books of poetry or philosophy, which sell in numbers too small to be noticeable on the scale used for TV audiences. Yet the above are all of vital importance to our cultural well-being and our future.

The Public Broadcasting Service would seem to be the answer to this problem in the United States. It exists to supply the needs of the by-no-means tiny minority of people who want to see Shakespeare, serious modern drama, documentaries, programs on the arts and sciences, and so forth. Yet so underfinanced and organizationally fragmented is this network that it cannot fulfill a fraction of these demands, even by relying heavily on BBC imports. Federal support of the Corporation for Public Broadcasting (which in turn funds the PBS) is barely able to help. In 1979 the total revenues of public broadcasting (radio and TV) amounted to some $600 million—about a fourth of which came from the federal government. That $600 million amounted to only about 5 percent of the total advertising revenue of the commercial television industry. In that year a single firm, Procter and Gamble, spent almost twice as much on TV advertising as the total sum the government appropriated to the Corporation for Public Broadcasting.

Corporate contributions are also insufficient to offset rising costs (and diminishing government support). Such corporate support is increasingly directed toward those programs with the widest popular appeal. It is, of course, an unfortunate fact that arts documentaries and Shakespearean plays cost more to produce than game shows or soap operas and that the results reach fewer people, making the cost of production per viewer spectacular. But it costs more to build and furnish a museum with paintings and sculpture by old masters than it does to build and equip a dance hall, and yet society manages to provide for both. It is only on the most powerful medium of mass communication that, in the United States, the coexistence of the popular and the minority taste seems impossible.

There are broadcasting systems in many other countries

that *do* allow for a coexistence of the popular and the minority tastes by planned alternative programming on parallel television channels. When a program with wide mass appeal is being shown on one channel, a program of narrower appeal will appear on the other, thereby satisfying both tastes at the same time. One of the drawbacks of commercialism in American television is this very lack of *variety* on the commercial channels, however numerous the channels themselves may be in metropolitan areas. If market research shows that at a given time in the afternoon the bulk of TV viewers will be housewives, then every commercial network enters the competition for soap, detergent, and cosmetic advertisements by showing what in their wisdom—or through scientific research—the program planners consider to be the right type of melodramatic serial for such an audience. The result: practically indistinguishable soap operas on all three main networks. The same applies to children's shows on Saturday mornings and even more so to the prime-time spots where situation comedy is pitted against situation comedy, adventure thriller against adventure thriller. This not only amounts to a neglect of minority tastes, it also deprives majority viewers of a genuine choice.

What is particularly disturbing about the narrowness of the intellectual range of American TV is that the U.S. truly needs a medium of mass communication and information that is available throughout the vast expanse of the nation. The absence of a national press, dictated as it is by geography, could be compensated for by a serious source of information available nationwide on TV. The three commercial networks do provide such a system, though of alarming uniformity, but apart from the very sparse national news programs and a few political documentaries and discussions, they neglect those areas where nationwide information would be of the greatest value: discussion of major ideological and social issues and information on the national culture. And the PBS, which tries to do the job, does not have sufficient resources to do it adequately. To me it is ironic that, for example, major American artistic achievements in the experimental theater like the work of Robert Wilson and The Bread and Puppet

Edith (Jean Stapleton) and Archie Bunker (Carroll O'Connor) on "All in the Family."

Theater are widely known in Europe and contribute to the reputation of American avant-garde art as among the best in the world, while in the United States they are virtually unknown outside the narrow confines of the areas in which they work.

There is more to this than merely the clamor of a few intellectuals to be supplied with programs they can enjoy. One of the most exhilarating aspects of our times is the possibility every individual now has of discovering his or her tastes, talents, and aptitudes through exposure to the activities and achievements of others in a nearly limitless variety of endeavors. The danger of targeting the intellectual and artistic level of television at the mentality of a twelve-year-old adolescent is that it is likely to impede the full intellectual and artistic development of individuals of promise. It is also likely to retard the reasoning power and tastes of the masses. The common argument that commercial TV gives people what they want is based on a fallacy. How can they desire material they have neither been shown nor offered? Experience has shown again and again that the minority tastes of today often become the majority tastes of tomorrow. Beethoven and Wagner were far-out avant-gardists when they started. A policy of giving the masses what is presently known to be their favorite fare by merely repeating successful formulas from the past tends to stagnate and fossilize popular entertainment and thus also the imagination of the majority of viewers. It is significant that several of the TV programs that have caught the American imagination—"All in the Family," for example, and "Sanford and Son"—are based on British television series which, when they started, were daring innovations with a minority appeal that later conquered a large audience. A prime function of the channels designed for minority viewing in countries like France, West Germany, and Britain is to experiment with new programming without being deterred by consideration of its immediate audience appeal.

The doctrine of giving the multitudes "what they want" can be seen to initiate a dangerous cycle of negative feedback, whereas a more open system, which allows the minorities their right of access to the most exciting medium of information, could reverse the vicious circle by injecting more innovative and more intelligent material into programming and lead to a gradual elevation of the general level of taste and discernment. In the future the impact of television on the minds and imaginations of men and women throughout the world will depend on whether ways and means can be found to widen the range television encompasses and to increase the sense of responsibility of those in control of this powerful medium. This leads us to the all-important question of *how* television can become subject to a more responsible form of control in the higher interest of society as a whole.

Detail from *Caliban* by Ben Shahn.

# 6

# Problems of Control

THE INVENTION OF THE PRINTING PRESS greatly increased man's capacity to communicate: information, facts, ideas, and opinions could be made available to far larger numbers of people at far lower costs than in previous epochs, when books had to be produced by scribes laboriously copying old manuscripts. It took a long time for the principle of freedom of the press to become established, however. Once this right was won in the more advanced countries of the Western world, this freedom became virtually limitless: almost anyone could get his ideas printed and distributed at relatively little expense. When the electronic mass media came into existence, they further enhanced mankind's capacity to communicate to even greater numbers at even greater speed. But they also presented a new and complex problem: there were only a limited number of channels available on the airwaves. If their number were increased above a certain limit, or their range increased by additional power, they would inevitably interfere with each other, there would be chaos, and the media's capacity to spread information and entertainment would break down altogether.

Strict regulation of the number, location, and power of broadcasting stations has thus been imperative from the day radio frequencies first began to be used to inform and entertain, in the early 1920s. Direct broadcasting over the airwaves—as distinct from distribution of the signals via cable or telephone lines—has always in all countries been subject to state regulation, and internationally to interstate negotiation and agreement. (When such control has failed, either through disregard of such agreements—as has happened internationally when countries of the Soviet bloc have increased the power of their propaganda stations far beyond the agreed limits—or through the discovery of a loophole in the law, which enabled television stations to sprout uncontrolled in Italy in the late 1970s, the consequences have always been highly disruptive.)

In the United States every radio and television station has to be licensed by the Federal Communications Commission (FCC). Established by Congress in 1934, and headed by seven commissioners appointed by the president with the consent of the Senate, the FCC is empowered to regulate all interstate and foreign communication by wire and radio, including telegraph, telephone, and broadcast. In this respect radio and television are as much under government control in the U.S. as they are elsewhere.

## Who Pays—and How?

From the outset, the necessity of government control of the distribution of wavelengths and strength of broadcasting stations and the limitation of the number of stations created a problem for free speech and expression over the open airwaves. There could be as many printed forms of communication as anyone wanted, but only a limited number of outlets for broadcast communication. To whom should that privilege be given? And once those fortunate enough to be allocated such a channel of communication began to broadcast, how were they to finance their programs? Broadcasts could be received at no charge by anyone with a set; they could not be sold individually to each recipient as could a newspaper, pamphlet, or book.

In the infancy of radio the manufacturers of radio sets

provided the programs at their own expense. They could not hope to sell their product unless they supplied something to be heard on the wonderful new contraptions. But after a while, when the thrill of hearing someone play a piano a hundred miles away had worn off, the public demanded more elaborate programming. And fulfilling that demand became ever more expensive.

Ways had to be found to finance the running and programming of radio stations. It is here that different solutions were found in Europe and in America.

*The British Model: the BBC*

In Britain the manufacturers of radio sets joined together to form the British Broadcasting Company, which began daily transmissions in November 1922. From the very beginning all listeners operating a radio set had to obtain a "broadcasting receiving license" (analogous to the license to operate a car in the United States and in most other countries). The license fee initially amounted to ten shillings (at that time two dollars) per annum. The general manager of the company was a young Scotsman, John Reith, the son of a clergyman, a brilliant administrator, and a person of the sternest moral fiber. Reith believed that so powerful a new instrument for informing, educating, and entertaining the masses as broadcasting was destined to be should be managed in the public interest, independent of interference from the state or business. To meet this requirement John (later Sir John, and later still Lord) Reith invented a new kind of public body: an organization established by the state but independent of it in its daily operation, and financed directly by its users through the license fee. On January 1, 1927, the new British Broadcasting *Corporation* was set up under a Royal Charter, originally designed to run for ten years and to be renewable by Parliament at regular intervals thereafter.

How was the BBC's independence from government interference to be achieved? The corporation is controlled by a board of governors who are appointed by the queen for five-year terms of office. Their number has varied over the years—it is twelve at present. The BBC's charter stipulates that there must be at least one governor for each of the three non-English nations of the United Kingdom: Scotland, Wales, and Northern Ireland; and it has also become a practice that among the rest of the board there are always governors representative of the trade unions, business, women, the academic world, and the arts. Once appointed, the board of governors, under its chairman, is sovereign in its responsibility over the corporation: it is empowered to use the license fee according to its own judgment and to appoint the chief executive of the corporation, the director general. The executive function of the board of governors stops here: it is not meant to interfere in the daily operation of the administration and of the programs on radio and television. The Royal Charter also forbids the BBC to raise any revenue by advertising.

The board of governors has to ensure that the BBC remains wholly impartial in political matters. A balance has to be maintained in the presentation of all responsible political views. During periods of general election campaigns the BBC has to allocate an agreed number of time slots for election broadcasts, which are provided by the political parties themselves and remain strictly outside the editorial control of the corporation (which, however, can be asked to furnish technical assistance in the form of studios, microphones, cameras, etc.). Between elections, similarly, there is an agreed number of "party political broadcasts" determined in a meeting of representatives of all the political parties in Parliament and on the basis of their strength in that body.

The Royal Charter of the BBC expressly specifies that the objective of the corporation is to disseminate "information, education and entertainment"—in that very significant order. The BBC thus regards itself as a public service with an important cultural and social role to play in the society.

The fixed license fee, which provided an ever-increasing and secure income while the number of radio sets continued to grow at leaps and bounds in the 1920s and 1930s, allowed the BBC to experiment not only in programming but also in technical innovation. It was the BBC that started the first regular daily television service in the world in 1936. To finance this fledgling TV service a television license fee was introduced. And as the number of television sets grew to saturation point, the radio license fee was abolished. Today some nineteen million British households pay a license fee amounting to some $90 for a color set, about $45 for a black-and-white set each year. That is to say, television costs the British household less than $2 per week for a color set, less than $1 for a black-and-white set. Compare this with the cost of television in the United States: in 1978 total revenues of all commercial stations in the U.S. amounted to some $7 billion; if one divides this sum by the roughly sixty million households in the country, the annual cost of television per household, which must come out of prices paid in the marketplace, also amounts to about $115—roughly $2.20 per week. The difference is that the BBC provides a service free from advertising and offering a much wider spectrum of programs.

The BBC as created by Reith became the model for most broadcasting organizations in Europe. Although commercial stations have also been licensed in most European countries (in Britain, for example, commercial television was introduced in 1954) and although some of the public broadcasting corporations in countries like France or Germany take a limited amount of advertising, the bulk of broadcasting expenses in Europe is still borne by the public broadcasting services. (In the Soviet-controlled parts of Europe, of course, all broadcasting is strictly government-run and controlled and merely an instrument of state propaganda.)

*The American Model*

In the United States the development of broadcasting followed a completely different pattern. It may well have been a mere accident of history that there happened to be no equivalent to John Reith in America and that the problem of who should pay for the programming on radio stations was solved—on the analogy of the daily press—by the sale of advertising time on the air.

The situation in the United States was also basically different from that in Europe in that the vast size of the United States made it much more difficult to develop a centralized broadcasting service for the whole country. The great distances between the major centers of population favored a much more localized approach. In the smaller countries of Europe there was less scope for local stations that would not interfere with each other (at least with the state of technology as it existed in the 1920s and 1930s, before the advent of FM). In the United States it was possible to allocate a large number of relatively low-powered stations to each major center of population. Nevertheless in radio—and later in television—a system of networking of the more ambitious program material had to develop simply because of the immense costs involved with producing high-standard programming, particularly in television. The U.S. system that evolved thus incorporated a considerable amount of local autonomy within a basic structure of three commercial networks financed entirely by advertising revenues.

So it came about that television in America became, in effect, a branch of the advertising industry. Whatever other qualities TV programs possess, they contribute to one basic purpose: to fill the gaps between advertisements, to induce people to turn on their sets so that they will see the advertisements. In his *New Yorker* profile of Johnny Carson, written in 1979, Kenneth Tynan quoted Carson as saying: "If you are selling hard goods—like soap or dog food—you simply can't afford to put on culture." One cannot put it more clearly or succinctly than that.

American commercial television, in generating enormous sums of money through advertising, has been immensely successful in producing programs of high technical quality and the widest popular appeal—not only within the U.S. but worldwide. However it has effectively abdicated any positive cultural function. The FCC, under its charter, is charged with the responsibility of interpreting "the public interest" in broadcasting. It also is empowered to remove broadcasting licenses from stations that have "demonstrably failed to serve the public interest, convenience or necessity." But in practice

Production shot from the PBS mini-series adaptation of Nathaniel Hawthorne's *The Scarlet Letter*. Photo: WGBH Educational Foundation.

these powers are hardly ever exercised. The concept of the public interest remains exceedingly vague and is rarely interpreted as meaning more than the provision of news, public announcements, or the granting of air time to spokesmen of various political bodies or pressure groups to voice their views in brief statements to be countered by their opponents on the basis of the principle of equal time.

The deficiencies of this state of affairs, which in 1961 the then-chairman of the FCC, Newton Minow, described as "the vast wasteland" of commercial television, were recognized officially by the establishment of the Public Broadcasting Service (PBS) through the Public Broadcasting Act, which became law in 1967. The PBS evolved out of the educational broadcasting stations that had tried to fill the arid stretches of the cultural wasteland in the 1950s. The PBS is, in effect, an alliance of local community and educational stations financed by grants from the Corporation for Public Broadcasting, also established by the 1967 Act, and supplemented by grants from the National Endowments for the Humanities and the Arts, funds from university sources, public subscriptions, and donations from the big corporations who regard sponsorship of culturally respectable programs as a form of discreet prestige advertising. Thus, while in theory there is no advertising on PBS, there is frequent mention of sponsoring corporations' names; and, in addition, the stations have to devote considerable time to soliciting voluntary subscriptions and gifts from their public. This necessitates frequent intrusions analogous to the commercials on the big networks, and emphasizes the dire financial straits public broadcasting has been in since its inception.

The congressional appropriation for public television through the Corporation for Public Broadcasting was set at $162 million for 1981. The appropriation proposed for the CPB in President Reagan's budget for 1982 is only about 75 percent of that sum. The total annual revenue of public broadcasting (television *and radio*) amounted to about $600 million in 1979. This compares with a total advertising revenue of commercial television and radio of more than *$12 billion* in the same year—that is to say commercial broadcasting was more than twenty times richer than public sector broadcasting, even before the implementation of the proposed drastic cuts in federal funding, which will extend beyond the reduction of the direct contribution from the CPB, as considerable funds come to PBS from the National Endowments for the Arts and the Humanities, whose federal funding is to be cut in half under the President's proposed 1982 budget.

Paucity of financial resources—basically crippling as it is— is by no means the only organizational weakness of the PBS. Its decentralized structure makes genuine networking of programs very difficult and thus deprives public TV of the great advantages of national publicity. Under this decentralized method of programming, initiating a new series entails a lengthy and cumbersome process by which a sufficient number of stations must be convinced to support such projects in advance. In the big public television organizations of Europe decisions of this nature can be swiftly and efficiently taken at the center. There are considerable advantages in size and concentration in television—as, indeed, is the case in the closely related film industry.

## Public TV: Drawbacks and Advantages

The European system of publicly controlled TV has its drawbacks, too. In Great Britain, for instance, the independence of the public broadcasting body does not extend to the critical aspect of the annual license fee. Although this fee is still relatively low, the government is reluctant to allow it to be raised too abruptly for fear of incurring public disfavor, even when inflation is rising at a steep rate. The government thus has an indirect means of exerting pressure on the BBC—which that organization up to now has fairly successfully withstood by publicly repudiating government attempts to interfere with programming, often with the result of angering the government of the day. In some European countries—Italy, France, and West Germany—there have been attempts at direct political interference in the editorial side of political reporting; but, on the whole, public control of broadcasting has worked in the West. In totalitarian regimes, including those in the Soviet bloc, the state controls all information media. The result, paradoxically, is a television system that is far less effective as political propaganda, and less popular as well, because it is utterly predictable and therefore boring. East Germans and Czechs along the borders, who can receive Western television, greatly prefer it to what they are offered on their side of the Iron Curtain.

What are the advantages and disadvantages of a public TV service as compared to a completely commercial system? One of the dangers inherent in a public service system is paternalism: some authority decides what the viewers should see and hear simply on the basis of what it arbitrarily feels would be good for them. Yet in countries where a highly developed public system exists alongside a commercial one, that danger is minimized because of the market pressure on the commercial system to give its audience what it wants. Indeed, in a dual system the danger is often that the public service may be tempted to ignore its stated purpose to serve the

PANDERING TO INTELLECTUALS

Drawing by Ziegler; © 1980
The New Yorker Magazine, Inc.

public interest and instead pander to mass preferences because of a sense of competition with the commercial networks.

Another problem that plagues public TV service is that it
may run short of money, which in turn can increase its dependence on the government. The extent of government
dependence is intimately connected to how the public broadcasting service is financed. In West Germany and Italy, for
example, the public broadcasting service takes advertising,
but it is usually confined to a clearly delimited area of the
network's programming. In Britain the BBC, as noted, relies
entirely on its annual license fee, which guarantees it a steady
income and allows long-term planning. In periods of severe
inflation, the license-fee system leaves the BBC in a dangerous position vis-a-vis the government, and the network's
income may decline in real terms. In countries where the
public broadcasting service is financed by an annual allocation

in the national budget, long-term planning becomes more difficult and the dependence on the government is far greater. Nevertheless public TV services financed on that pattern, such as the ABC in Australia and the CBC in Canada, provide programs of high quality that are genuine alternatives to the fare on the numerous popular and prosperous commercial networks. In Canada, this includes programs from the three commercial American networks.

One of the most important positive features of services under public control is their ability to provide planned, high-quality viewing alternatives. The BBC, for example, has two television channels, BBC 1 and BBC 2. The program planning on these two networks is closely coordinated so that highly popular material on one channel is regularly paired with more specialized and demanding fare on the other. And though the percentage of the audience that tunes in to the challenging programming may be small, the scale of magnitude operative in the mass media is such that even a small percentage of the viewing audience represents a very large number of people indeed. A popular dramatic series on BBC 1, for instance, may reach an audience of 20 percent of the adult population of Britain—about ten million people. A play by Shakespeare on BBC 2 that may attract an audience of only 5 percent nonetheless reaches about two-and-a-half million people—a substantial audience for a work of art. It would take a theater with a seating capacity of one thousand about seven years, or twenty-five hundred performances, to reach an equivalent number of people! Nor should it be overlooked that this audience will include people whose influence may be greater in the long run than that of the ten million who watched the entertainment program. In this system, no segment of the viewing public is forced to compromise with any other. In our example, not only did BBC 1 provide a popular entertainment program as an alternative to the Shakespeare, but, in addition, the commercial network offered still another popular program. By careful—perhaps paternalistic—planning the general audience satisfaction was substantially increased.

## The Virtues of a Mixed System

The argument against the supposedly paternalistic nature of publicly controlled television does not take into account that in countries with a free press, those who control the programs on the mass media are subject to constant observation and criticism. And as much or, as in the case of the BBC, *more* independent market research can be and is applied to the programming of public broadcasting services as to that of most commercial networks. In a democracy then, a genuinely mixed, pluralistic system seems to be the obvious solution to the problem of how best to control television programming.

Public and commercial television can coexist as equals, particularly if more stringent regulation of advertising practices is introduced. In many countries commercial networks are prohibited by law from filling more than a very limited number of minutes in each hour with commercials (in England it is seven minutes) and the commercials must come between programs ("in natural breaks" as the British law puts it) rather than at strategic intervals (crucial dramatic moments) during the program, as is the practice on American TV, where the TV Code allows a total of sixteen minutes of commercials per hour outside prime time and nine-and-a-half minutes in prime time.

In theory, the United States already has a mixed system. However, in practice, the Public Broadcasting Service has no stable financial base and has not yet succeeded in building up a network that can effectively and on an equal basis compete with the commercial system—equal in the sense of providing as full and well-balanced a service, complete with news, documentaries, drama, arts programs, etc., as do public service networks in other countries. The solution to the problem clearly lies in finding an acceptable basis for the financing of such a full public broadcasting system. If, as is usually argued, the license fee system so widely used and so fully accepted in Europe would be politically unacceptable in the United States, alternative means of funding could be found. A sales tax on all TV sets, for example, would yield

English soap opera into "masterpiece" for U.S. viewers: Ruby (Jenny Tomasin), Hudson (Gordon Jackson), and Mrs. Bridges (Angela Baddeley) in Masterpiece Theatre's "Upstairs, Downstairs." Photo: WGBH Educational Foundation.

substantial annual revenues; such an excise tax was suggested by the Carnegie Commission on Educational Broadcasting, which recommended creation of the PBS in 1967. Or there could be a special tax on the profits of the commercial networks to go the public system. Any of these methods of financing would be preferable to a direct government grant that has to be budgeted annually, which subjects public television service to direct political pressure.

In countries where a mixed system of control actually exists, the influence of the public broadcasting service on the commercial networks is as noticeable as the need for the public system to compete with the commercial networks in the more popular programming areas. In Britain, for example, serious drama and programs on the arts are regular programming features of the commercial network, in part because public service programming is a factor in the evaluation of applications for license renewals, due every seven years, but more importantly because the population has become used to these features and would regard a network not providing them as giving less than a full service—even if they are not to the taste of large numbers of viewers.

One of the difficulties of the American situation is that the size of the U.S. favors decentralization and the fragmentation of initiatives for the more ambitious programming of the public service network. A revitalized PBS would need a strong central governing body that could allocate to local producing stations the substantial sums of money they require for ambitious projects—projects that could compete with the best offerings of the rich commercial competitors.

### Cable and Pay TV: A Solution?

Today there is much talk about the emergence of cable television and pay television and how they will revolutionize TV. Cable television can provide individual households with a far larger number of channels than can broadcast TV and, as it is financed by a monthly subscription, cable TV should in theory be able to provide a much wider variety of programming with greater attention to minority tastes. Similarly, pay television, which offers viewers an opportunity to pay for an individual program (as they would pay for a movie seen at a theater), could derive considerable revenue from what now would be regarded as small minority tastes: a million viewers nationwide—a minute audience by the standards of the national TV ratings of today—might well not only finance a highly artistic play or film but even yield a handsome profit to its producers.

But if the relatively high cost of cable services is acceptable to large numbers of people, is this not then an equivalent of the European license-fee system? Not really: by limiting this enhanced service to those who are able and willing to pay for it, huge numbers of people who might benefit from such improved service would still be deprived of it. Thus the great potential long-term social and cultural benefits of a more sophisticated mass medium *available to all viewers* would be lost. The same drawback inheres in the pay-television concept: the large amounts of money that can be raised by charging viewers as much as they would pay for a movie ticket for a first-run film or an opera performance denies viewing access to those who cannot afford to pay. Again, the tremendous advantage of a broadcasting medium that is freely accessible to all is lost.

## Practical Possibility or Fantasy?

Using existing satellite technology, a truly national network of public service television could be made available to the entire country. If a public service television organization was able to provide simultaneous, alternative programming along the lines of BBC 1 and BBC 2, the cultural role of television in the United States could be radically improved, and the most powerful communication medium in history could realize its positive potential to inform, educate, and provide exposure to diverse cultural ideas.

Is such a solution within the realm of practical possibility, or is it pure fantasy? To me, one of the most astonishing aspects of the American scene is its parochialism about its broadcasting system. Commercial television, with all its faults, is regarded by otherwise enlightened and responsible citizens almost as part of the natural order of things, so that the very idea of an alternative does not even surface. Yet just a glance across the borders of the United States into Canada reveals the possibility of a system that though far from perfect is in many ways preferable. British visitors to the U.S. are regularly surprised to be asked, and with great frequency, "Why is British TV so good?" This question almost seems to spring from a conviction that some undefinable sensibility is found on that little island that is beyond the grasp of the U.S. Taking into account the great resources and talents of Americans, the reality is that a more rational method of financing programs that aim for artistic respectability would probably produce superior results equivalent to the best of British television. The American cinema, after all, has produced first-rate and highly artistic entertainment for decades.

Concerns about government control of TV must be taken seriously. Yet experience with forms of control that minimize that danger in other countries, from Britain to West Germany, from Norway to Switzerland, does show that while vigilance must always be exercised—which is perfectly feasible in any country with a free press—a public broadcasting service, in practice, can achieve a high degree of independence.

There remains always this vexing question of financing such a public service: assuming that one advocates an annual TV license fee or an excise tax, why should people who don't want to watch certain types of programs be required to pay for them? Yet people who do not have children pay taxes that finance public schools and universities; people who do not visit museums pay for them through their taxes. The question, then, becomes: is a rationally structured mass communications service—radio as well as TV—as vital to the well-being of the nation as are libraries, museums, schools, and universities?

The answer to me seems beyond doubt. The absence of an adequately funded public television service in the U.S. in an age when other nations are in a position to make much fuller use of the positive potential of so powerful a medium amounts to no less than a national tragedy. To say that nothing can be done about the status quo and act as if it is a fact of life that television should continue to be geared to the intellectual level of a twelve-year-old child is a mixture of abject defeatism and dispirited complacency. In a democracy there are vast possibilities when enough people of intelligence and determination become convinced that a change is necessary—and take the initiative to make those changes.

And this is the crux of the matter: if it is realized that the present condition of the mass communication media in the United States constitutes a calamitous deficiency and might well entail very real dangers for the future economic well-being as well as cultural creativity and general standing of the nation, then surely there is a case for doing something about it. I find it deeply depressing that Lawrence Lichty, the author of a thoughtful and concerned article on the state of television in America, "Success Story," in the Winter 1981 issue of the prestigious *Wilson Quarterly*, can say about this matter:

> One still reads, from time to time, laments in the press or in academic journals about what television "could have been," as if it could have been any different than what it actually became. Its future, as a mass marketing tool, was determined well before its birth, in a very Darwinian sense. A fish cannot fly; it swims.

This strikes me not only as false because highly parochial—radio and television did become different elsewhere—but also as horrifyingly defeatist. Had the same attitude been taken about slavery, civil rights, the status of women, we would still have slaves, still have segregation in hotels, restaurants, and buses, still have women as chattels of their husbands or fathers. Surely the essence of a democracy lies in its ability to change conditions that have been recognized as immoral, harmful, or degrading. What is essential is the will to effect such a change and the determination to make the masses of the people—who are in the last analysis capable of intelligent and wise insights—realize the need for such change. The wasteland of television is not an unalterable feature of the American landscape. It is man-made and therefore not beyond the range of determined social and political action.

*Rank* postscript to *34 Drawings for Dante's Inferno* by Robert Rauschenberg. 1964. Collection, The Museum of Modern Art, New York.

# 7

# The Challenge of the Future

HOW WILL FUTURE AGES view our own? Where, should we fail
to halt and reverse present trends of crisis and decline, will
generations to come locate the root causes of failure and
disaster? We need not be incurable pessimists if, from time
to time, we undertake the exercise of trying to extrapolate
present trends to their logical outcome: indeed, only if we
do this shall we be able to meet the challenge of the future.
What, then, a hundred or two hundred years hence might
posterity come to regard as the greatest American disaster
in the twentieth century? It may well turn out not to be the
Great Depression, or Pearl Harbor, or the Vietnam War, or
Watergate, or double-digit inflation, but, in fact, American
television, or rather the chain of historical accidents by which
the main medium of information and entertainment of the
century, so rich in its potential for the enlightenment of the
masses, for the raising of the level of culture and democracy,
was allowed to become a negative rather than a positive force
in society.

## TV: An Educational Resource

That television has become the principal medium of mass

communication and mass information is beyond doubt. So too is the fact that in this highly competitive age the continued well-being of any nation depends on the level of intelligence, inventiveness, awareness, and skill of an ever-larger proportion of its work force: we have entered the post-industrial age in which the unskilled blue-collar worker of the past is giving way to the white-collar intellectual-cum-scientist able to understand and operate the most sophisticated equipment.

This situation, basically, presents an immense challenge to the educational system of any modern society. Television, as the medium that reaches children even before they enter school and shapes their mental development as powerfully as does their schooling, the medium that plays such a critical role in determining the intellectual and cultural environment of the whole society, must in this context be regarded as an essential ingredient in any nation's educational system. It surely cannot be a matter of indifference if so vital a sector of a nation's cultural organism remains geared to a major objective totally unrelated to such considerations—namely, the maximizing of the audience for advertisements, an objective moreover that willy-nilly tends to lower rather than raise levels of awareness and intelligence. There is a truly tragic dimension to this conflict between what, on the one hand, are obviously vital concerns of the society and, on the other, society's failure to make use of its principal medium of mass communication and enlightenment to deal with these concerns. It would be as if, a century earlier, the United States had tried to live through the age of industrialization without having a serious press to speak of, conducting its political debate simply through comic strips and cartoons.

The analogy may seem farfetched, the diagnosis unduly harsh. But a situation in which the majority of a population receives its principal intellectual stimulus, its food for thought, its value system, from a medium catering to the mentality of an adolescent cannot but be a disaster. Can a major nation survive on babytalk? Can reality be mastered by a population nurtured on daydreams?

Some of the dangers inherent in the present situation stem

from the nature of television itself, its difficulty in dealing with abstract ideas as efficiently as does the written word, its tendency to turn everything into drama, its emphasis on personality and the more superficial aspects of personality at that. But all these tendencies might, at least to some extent, be countered by judicious use and control of the medium. It is here that the United States falls short of most other countries of the Western world.

Granted that television is *the* popular art form of our day, that most TV programming must be a reflection of the collective unconscious and the hidden primitive aspirations of the masses; deliberate and judicious use can nonetheless be made of TV's artistic potential—as a dramatic medium of great power—and of its admittedly limited ability to convey hard facts and important information.

### The Television We Deserve?

Of course, television must always be examined and judged within the context of the whole cultural environment. Television reflects the level of the national culture while in turn contributing to the shaping of it. Any democratic, developed country will in the long run have the television it deserves. Efforts to improve television will have to be made within the much wider context of the educational system as a whole. In its widest sense this includes not only schools and universities, but also museums, libraries, the press, the arts, and the entire infrastructure that underlies the nation's cultural consciousness and self-image.

The broadening of the base of the educational system far beyond the bounds achieved by the elitist societies of Europe has been one of the major achievements and chief glories of the revolutionary American political system. But the broadening of the base has also led to a weakening and lowering of standards. The present-day demand for more rigorous educational standards, for stricter attention to the acquisition of and achievement in the basic skills—reading, writing, and arithmetic—is an indication of a growing awareness that we are at the threshold of a new phase of democratic advance in education where, building on the foundation of the newly achieved quantitative advance, the emphasis must now be shifted to the *quality* of the education these vast numbers of people actually receive. And it is in this context that we must examine the role that television currently plays in the educational experience of virtually every child in the country, as well as the role that it is bound to play in the intellectual and emotional development of the adult population. For in a society undergoing such rapid technological change as ours is, the educational process cannot possibly end with the end of schooling.

## A Rational Role for Television

In any reassessment of the overall need for change in the educational system the electronic mass media will thus have to occupy a crucial position, for they are now, for better or worse, part and parcel of that system. Once the nature of television and its limitations and strengths as a dramatic medium are fully recognized, basic changes can be instituted in TV programming. A rational use of the medium would then concentrate on raising the artistic level of dramatic programs and would employ their attractiveness as storytelling devices to strengthen gradually their intellectual content through the dramatization of social and ideological problems, while at the same time raising levels of taste in the field of visual design. Such a rational use of television would have to be preceded by an intelligent assessment of the electronic media as a whole. Radio can do many things better than television, though at present it often fails to do them. As a purely verbal and aural medium, radio is better able to convey abstract thought than is TV. Radio can be used effectively as a literary medium, as a vehicle for conveying scientific information, or as a forum for serious political debate. In an era in which so much emphasis is placed on oral communication, the educational system will have to redouble its efforts to increase not only literacy but also serious reading. And as previously noted television has demonstrated its ability to arouse interests that are later satisfied by reading. In certain areas of children's television it has been shown that it is possible to *activate* children through the medium rather than turn them into passive, zombielike consumers. Programs like "Sesame Street" have demonstrated the creative and educationally effective use of television.

## TV Criticism: A Required Subject

The educational system in a television age must teach students how to view TV critically, with intelligence and discrimination. *Television criticism,* whether under that title or another, should become a basic subject of instruction in schools from the earliest grades. How would such a subject be taught? On the elementary level, it would start with a basic description of TV's technical background; this would make students aware of the fact that most television, even the seemingly spontaneous, is *staged,* that the "solitary" speaker or "spontaneous event" is in fact surrounded by cameramen and sound men, production assistants and directors. Students would be shown what goes on behind the scenes of a production studio so that they could get an idea of what is actually happening while they watch the screen. There could be discussion of the organizational structure of television as a whole, its financing, its dependence on advertising, the nature of advertising techniques and psychology. And then, at higher grades, there would be an application of the methods of dramatic criticism to the assessment and evaluation of TV programs. A trained, knowledgeable audience would, inevitably, have a positive effect on the standards of programming.

## An Ideal Solution?

The creation of such a critically aware audience must go hand in hand with a strengthening of the range and quality of what is being offered on the television screen itself. The commercial system is so deeply entrenched, so highly popular, and so bound up with powerful vested interests that any thought of a radical modification of the commercial net-

Violinist Itzhak Perlman joins Oscar the Grouch in a rare performance on "Sesame Street" of Johan Sebastian Blech's "Double Sonata for Violin, Vacuum Cleaner, Policeman's Whistle, Fire Engine Siren, Jackhammer, Automobile Horn, Elephant Jumping into Pool and Nose." Perlman, asked to comment on the duet, said, "it fulfilled my wildest dreams." Photo: Courtesy of Children's Television Workshop.

works is clearly not feasible. Nor, indeed, would it be desirable. On the other hand, a strengthening of the already existing public television system is wholly within the technical and financial capabilities of the nation.

A public service network, preferably one able to broadcast on two nationally accessible alternative channels—as is the case with the public networks in Britain, France, West Germany, Italy, and most other Western European countries, where public networks exist side by side with commercial systems—would provide a legitimate alternative to the commercial system. To suggest such a solution at a time when radical cuts are being made in the financing of the existing impoverished public service system may seem highly unrealistic. Yet all that is needed is a sufficiently strong awareness of the urgency and importance of the matter among a large enough sector of the electorate to put an end to the prevailing mood of complacency that regards any change in the status quo as beyond the bounds of political practicality. Here the very triviality of American television is at the root of public apathy. Why should one get agitated about something so silly, so trivial, as television?

Of such complacency are great national disasters compounded. For it is the triviality of television as it now *is* that masks and conceals the potential of television as it *might be* in such a vital and concerned democracy. Information is the lifeblood of any democracy. The misuse or nonuse of the principal information medium, placed at mankind's disposal by a tremendous technological advance, thus amounts to a self-inflicted wound upon democracy.

## A Vicious Circle

But here we confront a vicious circle of events. In a democracy social changes that are desired by a sufficiently large number of people usually can be brought about over a period of time. But how can people want what they do not know? How can they clamor for something of which they remain unaware? This is the principal irony, and misfortune, of the media situation in the United States. It springs to a large extent from the self-sufficiency of a country so large and powerful that it sees little need to look beyond its own frontiers, an aspect of that cultural parochialism that leads to a neglect of the study of foreign languages, let alone foreign civilizations, and has already had some dire political consequences, such as the underestimation of the sophistication of the French-educated Vietnamese leadership in the Vietnam War. It is this refusal to become aware of the potential of television as a means to raise the cultural level of the nation that lies at the root of what to an outsider must appear a willful neglect of the proper use of a vital technological advance. It is a state of affairs that—*mutatis mutandis*—seems analogous to the situation in which the Chinese knew of the existence of gunpowder but for centuries regarded it merely as a toy for entertainment, to be employed in creating spectacular fireworks. They were to pay heavily for ignoring the less frivolous potential of their discovery when they encountered Europeans who used the same technology for military purposes—to establish political ascendancy over China that endured for centuries.

Recognition of the importance of the television medium in the educational system and a spread of that awareness throughout the population should be, in my view, one of the top priorities on the nation's agenda. There is, of course, a paradox operating here: the spread of such an awareness is a matter of communication; and it is precisely the system of mass communications that is controlled by forces that would be implacably opposed to the spread of such an awareness. But even here, the situation is not hopeless. And, powerful as the electronic mass media are, there are still alternative channels of communication open: a free press, public meetings, public discussion, and the state and federal legislative bodies themselves.

### Releasing Creative Energy

The opening up of the mass media to serious thought, serious drama, and serious art would release an immense amount of new creative energy by providing a training

Behind the scenes.

ground, as it does already in Europe, for writers, directors, actors, and designers whose work can enrich the stage and the cinema as well. Similarly there is great scope for serious documentary filmmakers. Television, with its topicality and immediacy, is an ideal vehicle for documentary films—a branch of the cinema that has regressed considerably from the glorious days of its flowering in the period before and during World War II.

Intellectually demanding television will never be popular with the great masses of the population. But experience in other countries indicates that about 10 percent of the population does want such fare—in the United States that would amount to some *twenty-three million people* who are now practically disenfranchised from the most powerful and efficient medium of communication and information. And it is on the creativeness, inventiveness, and leadership of that minority that the intellectual, cultural, and *economic* well-being of the nation principally depends, for that minority comprises the inventors and designers, the policymakers and policy planners, the teachers and leaders in any community. And these people do not exist in isolation. The electronic media, once they are geared to provide this material, would also make it readily available to anyone who happened to find himself or herself interested in it. The widest possible range of intellectual and artistic material of the highest caliber on television would attract new creative blood to the existing audience for such programming, as well as provide a constant challenge to the commercial networks, which would have to take this competition into account. This, indeed, happens already in countries where high-level public service television coexists with commercial programming.

### Freedom to Choose

The provision of a source of programs of the highest artistic and intellectual standards in sufficient quantity and with the widest possible range of subject matter would significantly enlarge the intellectual freedom of the nation. One aspect of freedom, after all, is the freedom to choose—the potential to select among a wide and genuine range of alternatives. In the realm of the printed word that freedom exists, at least in theory. (In practice, it is restricted by the paucity of good bookstores and libraries in some areas.) In recent decades that freedom has greatly shrunk in the daily press because of the death of alternative newspapers in many important population centers. But it still remains at least in the field of weekly and monthly and quarterly periodicals that are available in abundance. In the electronic mass media in their present state that freedom can hardly be said to exist at all. And yet it is in the area of the electronic media that the freedom to choose among a broad range of genuine alternatives is needed most.

It is through television that most young people in our society first encounter the world of culture in the widest sense, that their first tastes are formed—or indeed distorted and deadened. Nobody should be compelled to like the greatest art, the highest flights of the intellect, but everyone should at least have an opportunity to encounter them. *Denial of access* to these areas of human achievement on the most generally accessible medium of communication amounts to the denial of a basic human right. An extension of television to encompass the whole range of cultural activity must thus be regarded as, above all, the reestablishment of one of the greatest and most vital of human liberties.

# READER'S GUIDE

The literature on broadcasting in general and television in particular is vast. It is also extremely uneven. In the subject catalogues of libraries, show-business gossip is stacked next to strictly scientific works on electronic communications technology, advertising manuals next to violent denunciations of commercialism. And there is also a considerable amount of behaviorist psychology trying to quantify the unquantifiable.

In the United States there are a number of useful reference works that give the basic statistics on viewing figures, set ownership, and the current status of regulation of the industry. Among these are:

- *The Media Book* (published annually; New York: Min-Mid Publishing).
- *International Television Almanac, 1980,* edited by R. Gertner (New York: Quigley Publishing, 1980).
- *The New York Times Encyclopedia of Television,* edited by L. Brown (New York: Times Books, 1977).
- C.S. Steinberg, *TV Facts* (New York: Facts on File, 1980).
- C.T. and P.G. Norback, *TV Guide Almanac* (New York: Ballantine Books, 1980).

A good survey of the history of American television is provided by E. Barnow in *Tube of Plenty: The Evolution of American Television* (New York: Oxford University Press, 1975).

Television as a business is discussed in:

- L. Brown, *Television: The Business Behind the Box* (New York: Harcourt Brace Jovanovich, 1971).
- R. Adler and W.S. Baer, *The Electronic Box Office* (New York: Praeger, 1974).

Television and its treatment of politics and the news are critically described in:

- E. Diamond, *The Tin Kazoo: Television, Politics and the News* (Cambridge, Mass.: MIT Press, 1975).
- E. Efron, *The News Twisters* (Los Angeles: Nash, 1971).
- E.J. Epstein, *News from Nowhere: Television and the News* (New York: Vintage, 1974).
- F.W. Friendly, *Due to Circumstances Beyond our Control . . .* (New York: Random House, 1967).

And the full onslaught of critical condemnation against the medium is unleashed by J. Mander in *Four Arguments for the Elimination of Television* (New York: William Morrow, 1978).

Information about the main alternative system of broadcasting, the British, can be obtained from:

- *The BBC Handbook* (published annually; London: BBC Publications).
- *Independent Broadcasting Authority: Annual Report and Accounts* (London: Independent Broadcasting Authority).

The history of the BBC is given in great detail in A. Briggs's monumental work, *The History of Broadcasting in the United Kingdom*, four volumes (Oxford: Oxford University Press, 1961–79).

Public broadcasting in the United States owes its present form to the work of the Carnegie Commission on Educational Broadcasting. Its report is available as a book, *Public Broadcasting: A Program for Action* (New York: Harper & Row, 1967). Twelve years later the Carnegie Corporation convened a second commission, which advocated a reorganization of the PBS in a more centralized form and with funding that would reach $1.2 billion annually by 1985, including a federal contribution amounting to $630 million. The arguments for this proposal—which, from the moment of its conception seemed utopian—are contained in *A Public Trust: The Report of the Carnegie Commission on the Future of Public Broadcasting* (New York: Bantam Books, 1979).

A history of the early years of the PBS can be found in *To Irrigate a Wasteland* (Berkeley: University of California Press, 1974) by J.R. Macy, Jr., the first president of the Corporation for Public Broadcasting.

The first, and still fascinating, attempts to evolve a philosophy of the age of mass media are contained in Marshall McLuhan's *The Gutenberg Galaxy* (Toronto: University of Toronto Press, 1962) and *Understanding Media* (New York: McGraw-Hill, 1964).

A summary of the very bulky literature on the effects of sex and violence in the mass media and a full bibliography of the literature on that subject can be found in H.J. Eysenck and D.K.B. Nias's *Sex, Violence and the Media* (London: Maurice Temple Smith, 1978).

Among other important studies of the impact of television are:

- *The Uses of Mass Communications: Current Perspectives on Gratification Research,* edited by J.G. Blumler and E. Katz (Beverly Hills: Sage Publications, 1974).
- G. Comstock and others, *Television and Human Behavior* (New York: Columbia University Press, 1978).
- U.S. Commission on Obscenity and Pornography, *The Report of the Commission on Obscenity and Pornography* (New York: Bantam Books, 1970).

Useful books on the influence of television on children are:

- National Science Foundation, *Research on the Effects of Television Advertising on Children: A Review of the Literature and Recommendations for Future Research* (Washington, D.C.: National Science Foundation, 1977).
- U.S. Public Health Service, *Television and Growing Up: The Impact of Televised Violence. Report to the Surgeon General* (Washington, D.C.: U.S. Public Health Service, 1972).
- F.E. Barcus, *Children's Television: An Analysis of Programming and Advertising* (New York: Praeger Publishers, 1977).
- D. Cater and S. Strickland, *TV Violence and the Child: The Evolution and Fate of the Surgeon General's Report* (New York: Russell Sage Foundation, 1975).
- *Children and Television,* edited by R. Brown (Beverly Hills: Sage Publications, 1976).

An amusing account of the production of a television commercial, originally published in *The New Yorker,* is now available in book form in M.J. Arlen's *Thirty Seconds* (New York: Farrar, Straus & Giroux, 1980).

Another revealing *New Yorker* profile is that of Johnny Carson in K. Tynan's *Show People* (New York: Simon & Schuster, 1979).

A useful collection of articles on the present state of the medium is published under the title "Television in America" in *The Wilson Quarterly,* Winter 1981 (Washington, D.C.: Woodrow Wilson International Center for Scholars, 1981).

# ABOUT THE AUTHOR

For thirty-seven years—from 1940 to 1977—Martin Esslin worked with the British Broadcasting Corporation in London. He was born in Hungary and raised in Austria, where he studied at Vienna University (English and philosophy) and graduated from the Max Reinhardt Seminar of Dramatic Art, one of the foremost theater schools of Europe. After the Nazi occupation of Vienna in March 1938, he moved to England.

In England Esslin worked for the BBC as a translator, scriptwriter, and director in the wartime German department (which conducted the media war against Goebbels' propaganda) and later as a scriptwriter and assistant head in the European productions department. In 1960 he became assistant head of the BBC's radio drama department and in 1963 head of radio drama, a position he held until 1977 when he accepted an appointment as professor in the drama department at Stanford, where he now teaches for two quarters each year.

In 1972 Esslin, a drama critic of international renown, was awarded the O.B.E. (Officer of the Order of the British Empire) by Queen Elizabeth II for "service to broadcasting." In 1968 he won the Adolf Grimme Prize for scripting the best television arts program of that year in West Germany. He has served for many years as a member of the Drama Panel of the Arts Council of Great Britain and in 1976 acted as chairman. Esslin has written many books on the theater, among them *Brecht: The Man and His Work, Harold Pinter: A Study of His Plays, An Anatomy of Drama, Antonin Artaud,* and *Mediations.* His best-known book, *The Theatre of the Absurd,* gave coinage to that now-familiar phrase. The book has been translated into ten languages.

Esslin is a collector of books and records and is an avid radio listener and television viewer. He enjoys a life divided between Stanford—in the first half of the year—and Britain, where he lives in London but spends as much time as possible at his home in the picturesque, ancient country town of Winchelsea, on the Sussex coast. He is married and has one daughter, who at present is studying classics at Oxford.

# CREDITS

PAGE viii    Brauner, Victor. *Spread of Thought*. 1956. Oil on canvas. 28¾″ × 23½″. Collection, The Solomon R. Guggenheim Museum, New York. Gift of Mr. and Mrs. Jean de Menil, Houston, 1958. Photo: Robert E. Mates.

PAGE 5    Rauschenberg, Robert. *Mark* postscript to *34 Drawings for Dante's Inferno*. 1964. Lithograph, printed in black. Comp.: 14″ × 16¼″, Sh.: 15¾″ × 16¼″. Collection, The Museum of Modern Art, New York. Gift of Celeste and Armand Bartos Foundation.

PAGE 11    Jack Ruby about to fire point-blank into Lee Harvey Oswald's abdomen. © 1963 The Dallas Morning News. Photo: Wide World Photos, New York.

PAGE 12    Astronaut Edwin Aldrin on the moon's surface during the Apollo II EVA, 1969. Photo: Courtesy of NASA/Ames Research Center, Moffett Field, California.

PAGE 14    Johnny Carson as Carnac the Magnificent on "The Tonight Show." Photo: Courtesy of NBC, Burbank, California.

PAGE 16    Francesca Annis as Lillie Langtry in Masterpiece Theatre's "Lillie." Photo: WGBH Educational Foundation, Boston.

PAGE 25    Laurence Olivier as Hamlet with Basil Sydney as Claudius in *Hamlet*. Courtesy of The Rank Organization Limited, London. Photo: National Film Archive/Stills Library, London.

PAGE 28    Desi Arnaz and Lucille Ball in a breakfast scene from "I Love Lucy." Photo: Culver Pictures.

PAGE 31    "We're at the home of Jim and Mindy Marks, who are about to discover that their utility bill has gone sky-high. Let's watch." Drawing by Maslin; © 1980 The New Yorker Magazine, Inc.

PAGE 34    Jack Palance and Kim Hunter in Rod Serling's "Requiem for a Heavyweight" on "Playhouse 90." From *A Pictorial History of Television* by Irving Settel and William Laas. © 1969 Irving Settel and William Laas. Courtesy of Grosset & Dunlap, Inc., New York.

PAGE 40    Blackthorne (Richard Chamberlain), Lady Mariko (Yoko Shimada), and Lord Toranaga (Toshiro Mifune) in the TV mini-series adaptation of James Clavell's *Shogun*. Photo: Courtesy of the National Broadcasting Company, Inc. Copyright © 1980 NBC.

PAGE 47    Shirley (Cindy Williams) and Laverne (Penny Marshall) on "Laverne & Shirley." Photo: Copyright © 1981, courtesy of Paramount Pictures.

PAGE 52    Superman saves the day on "The Superfriends Hour." Superman is a registered trademark of DC Comics Inc. and is used by permission. Copyright © 1981 DC Comics Inc.

PAGE 56    Chicago police and dissenting youths during riots that disrupted the 1968 Democratic National Convention. From *A Pictorial History of Television* by Irving Settel and William Laas. © 1969 Irving Settel and William Laas. Courtesy of Grosset & Dunlap, Inc., New York.

PAGE 60    A starving Kampuchean child. Photo: United Press International, New York.

PAGE 63 "Don't you understand? This is life, this is what is happening. We can't switch to another channel." Drawing by Robt. Day; © 1970 The New Yorker Magazine, Inc.

PAGE 64 American hostages shown being paraded by their militant Iranian captors on the first day of occupation of the U.S. Embassy in Tehran, November 4, 1979. Photo: United Press International, New York.

PAGE 67 Anchorman Walter Cronkite on "CBS Evening News." Photo: Courtesy of CBS, New York.

PAGE 74 Demonstrators en route to an anti-Vietnam War rally at San Francisco's Kezar Stadium, April 1972. Photo: United Press International, New York.

PAGE 76 Drawing by Paul Conrad. Copyright © 1979, Los Angeles Times. Reprinted with permission.

PAGE 79 Kunta Kinte (LeVar Burton) in the TV mini-series adaptation of Alex Haley's *Roots*. "Roots," a David L. Wolper Production. Photo: Courtesy of The Wolper Organization, Inc., Burbank, California.

PAGE 83 Eros (Simon Chandler) and Anthony (Colin Blakely) in *Anthony and Cleopatra* on "The Shakespeare Plays," produced by BBC-TV/Time-Life Television. Photos from the BBC/Time-Life coproduction of "The Shakespeare Plays." Courtesy of the Exxon Corporation, Metropolitan Life Insurance Company, and Morgan Guaranty Trust.

PAGE 88 Rauschenberg, Robert. *Merger*. 1962. Lithograph, printed in black. Comp.: 13⅞" × 11⅛", Sh.: 22½" × 17½". Collection, The Museum of Modern Art, New York. Gift of Celeste and Armand Bartos Foundation.

PAGE 94 Edith (Jean Stapleton) and Archie Bunker (Carroll O'Connor) on "All in the Family." © 1980 by Tandem Productions, Inc. All rights reserved.

PAGE 96 Shahn, Ben. Detail from *Caliban*. 1953. Serigraph. 25½" × 39". © Estate of Ben Shahn 1981. Photo: Courtesy of *The Wilson Quarterly*, Washington, D.C.

PAGE 103 Production shot from the PBS mini-series adaptation of Nathaniel Hawthorne's *The Scarlet Letter*. Photo: Robert Philippe for WGBH; WGBH Educational Foundation, Boston.

PAGE 106 *Pandering to Intellectuals*. Drawing by Ziegler; © 1980 The New Yorker Magazine, Inc.

PAGE 109 Ruby (Jenny Tomasin), Hudson (Gordon Jackson), and Mrs. Bridges (Angela Baddeley) in Masterpiece Theatre's "Upstairs, Downstairs." Photo: WGBH Educational Foundation, Boston.

PAGE 114 Rauschenberg, Robert. *Rank* postscript to *34 Drawings for Dante's Inferno*. 1964. Lithograph, printed in black. Comp.: 14" × 16", Sh.: 15¹¹⁄₁₆" × 16". Collection, The Museum of Modern Art, New York. Gift of Celeste and Armand Bartos Foundation.

PAGE 120 Violinist Itzhak Perlman joins Oscar the Grouch for a rare performance on "Sesame Street." Photo: Courtesy of Children's Television Workshop, New York.

PAGE 123 Behind the scenes. From *Both Sides of the Camera*, edited by Marie Donaldson. © 1960 ABC Television Limited, London. Courtesy of Weidenfeld and Nicolson, London. Photo: John Timbers.

PAGE 132 Martin Esslin. Photo: Chuck Painter, Stanford University.

# INDEX

Commercials (continued)
Carson, Johnny on, 102
as drama, 15
fantasy of, 72
mental level targets of, 85
patterns in, 48–54
real person presentations, 50
research on, 2–3
Saturday morning, 93
structure, 50
Common Market, news reporting
on, 61
Control of TV. *See* Regulation of
TV
Corporate contributions to PBS, 92
Corporation for Public
Broadcasting, 104
Costumes, 21
Creative TV, 122, 124
*Crime and Punishment*, 82
Critical approach to TV, 119
Cultural imperialism, 90

Daydream machine, 32–33
Democratic Convention, 1968, 56
Deus ex machina in commercials,
49, 50
Discussion programs, 70–71
Documentaries, 68–70
Dramatic medium, 6–7
Dramatis personae, 27–32
Dream factory, 32
Dubbing shows, 89–90
Duchamp, Marcel, 8

East German TV, 89
Editorial opinions, 29
Educational resource, TV as,
115–117
Entertainment principle, 61–65
Erotic appeal of TV, 32
European Economic Community,
61

False consciousness, 72–74
Family myth, 46
*Fausse conscience*, 72
*Faust*, 57–58
FCC. *See* Federal Communications
Commission

Federal Communications
Commission (FCC), 98
public interest, interpretation of,
102–103
Figure skating, 71
Foreign countries, American TV
in, 87–90
Format of series, 41
France, American TV in, 89

Game shows, 13, 15
dramatis personae, 27
personalities on, 29, 70–71
Gielgud, John, 23
Global village, 3
Goethe, 57–58
*The Golden Bowl*, 39
Gossip, 29–30
Grammar on TV, 6–10
Grumberg, Jean-Claude, 57

*Hamlet*, 8
personalities in, 22–23
reading of, 24
suspension of disbelief, 33
Heroes of TV, 44–46
Hostages in Iran, 64
Humanity in drama, 84
Huxley, Aldous, 1

Ice dancing, 71
"I Love Lucy," 28
Images, 22
Interview programs, 70–71
Iranian hostage situation, 64

Jackson, Gordon, 109

Kampuchea, famine in, 59, 60
Keaton, Buster, 42
Kennedy, John, 11
*King Lear*, 82

Language of TV, 6–10
Laurel and Hardy, 43
"Laverne & Shirley," 47
License fee for BBC, 100–101
Lichty, Lawrence, 113
Lighting plot, 21
Literature, 23–27